TITLETOWN

The Green Bay Packers' Unforgettable Road to
Super Bowl XXXI

Green Bay
Press-Gazette

Acknowledgements

RESEARCH ASSISTANCE: Sue Kluck, Green Bay Packers; Claude Werder, John Morton, Dian Robb, Pat Ferron, Joe Heller, Laurie Holloway, Kathy Tett and Laurie Vicenzi, the *Green Bay Press-Gazette*; NFL Properties; Wide World Photo; Allsport Photography USA; Jim Russ and Steve Fecht, *The Detroit News*.

PRODUCTION ASSISTANCE: Susan Kordalski, Amy Kinsella and Rick Epps.

ISBN 1-887761-17-9

COVER AND BOOK DESIGN: David Kordalski, Detroit.
TYPFACES: Life, Village, Bureau Grotesque

PUBLISHED BY:
AdCraft Sports Marketing
Kaden Tower, 10th Floor
6100 Dutchmans Lane
Louisville, KY 40205
(502) 473-1124

*For other sports publications in the AdCraft library, call toll-free (888) 232-7238
or contact our web site at www.sport-mall.com*

Dedication

To the many loyal Green Bay
Packers fans — the best in the
National Football League

Contents

The Title is Back In Titletown

The Title is back in Titletown. The Green Bay Packers are World Champions once again. The long absent Vince Lombardi Trophy has been returned, and Packers fans everywhere can feel the change.

This book, *Titletown: The Unforgettable Story of the Green Bay Packers' Road to Super Bowl XXXI,* chronicles many of the changes the Packers experienced during their season-long march to Super Bowl XXXI. But Packers history is built on changes.

Andy Turnbull, the first publisher of The Press-Gazette, was also the first president of the Green Bay Packers.

He probably knew very little about running a football operation, but it was his idea to gather a number of business cronies together in his office to enlist their support in forming a pro football team. One of the contributors owned a meat packing plant and got naming rights, and Turnbull began his part-time job as president.

The Packers current president, Bob Harlan, is full-time and fully focused. He knows everything about running a first-class football team and has surrounded himself with the best in the business that help make it the envy of pro sport franchises.

The early Packer players tended to be slightly built. They wore few pads and relied mostly upon speed. Their namesakes were big, brawny men capable of hauling meat carcasses around on their shoulders.

Today's meat packers rely on automation to do the heavy lifting, while the players routinely move live 300 pound carcasses around, usually against their will.

My earliest Packer memories are from the old City Stadium in the fall of 1952.

I don't remember any game details, but if the weather wasn't uncomfortable, the games were an enjoyable way for a 7-year-old kid to spend a Sunday afternoon, probably because there was always popcorn and a soda.

My most recent Packers memory is only hours old. Every game detail is vividly framed with indescribable euphoria. It took place in a dome, where the weather is never uncomfortable, in a city named New Orleans, far from the memory of old wooden bleachers in City Stadium. There wasn't time for popcorn or soda, but what a glorious way to spend a Sunday evening.

My dad's acquisition of 10 season tickets in the early 1950's was driven partly by his support for the local team, but more so because he was a soft touch. During those years, local high school cheerleaders visited Green Bay companies selling Packers season tickets to help raise money for their school. They only got

paid for new orders, not renewals, so Dad kept increasing his order until every one of us had tickets. I guess there's something to be said for large families.

Tickets are no longer peddled door-to-door. The current waiting list for season tickets is estimated to extend beyond 40 years.

The changes go on and on, from nostalgia to current reality, from an unprofitable sport to a multi-million dollar business, from a forgotten team to the envy of the NFL.

Yet, in spite of all the changes, one constant has remained unchanged — a love affair between fans and players.

Andy Turnbull hatched the love affair in his office that day more than 75 year's ago, and it's been growing ever since.

This love affair goes well beyond fan adoration. It endures, through good years and bad, and is successful because it's mutual.

Reggie White summed it up with his comment to the 60,000 fans in Lambeau field following the NFC championship victory over the Carolina Panthers. "Green Bay, I hope you're proud of us, because we're proud of you," White said.

I hope some things never change. Enjoy the book.

BILL NUSBAUM
PUBLISHER
PRESS-GAZETTE
JAN. 27, 1997

Desmond Howard does the Lambeau Leap following his punt return for a touchdown against the Niners in the playoffs.

Gotta Love The Pack

By Kim Estep
Press-Gazette

GREEN BAY — With the temperature at 3 degrees and the wind chill at 17 below, Lawrence Luther's fingers were beginning to look like cherry popsicles a half hour before kickoff at Lambeau Field.

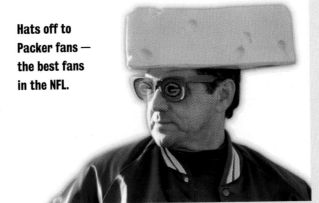

Hats off to Packer fans — the best fans in the NFL.

It was a Sunday, the day of the NFC championship game. The Green Bay Packers were host to the Carolina Panthers.

But Luther, an electrical contractor from Cecil, had no tickets.

He was at Lambeau because ... well ... simply because he wanted to be there. He would watch the game on a TV in the back of his van in the stadium parking lot.

This is the type of thing a Packer fan will do in Green Bay. These fans are crazy in love with their Packers.

These are folks who place volunteer-made green and gold caps on their newborns' noggins in the hospital.

These are folks who choose green and gold caskets to rest in peace, amen.

These are folks who wear — with pride — yellow wedges of foam on their heads.

These are folks who paint their bodies green with yardlines to resemble Lambeau Field.

These are folks in love.

Irene Olson remembers the early years.

The Packers played in City Stadium, now swallowed up by Green Bay East High School's land.

Olson first attended a game in 1935, paying 25 cents to watch Curly Lambeau coach a rookie from Alabama — that "southern gentleman," end Don Hutson.

She was hooked. On Hutson and the Packers.

"I saw Don Hutson go up for a pass with five other guys and come down with it," she said. "That day I thought they were just wonderful and heroic, especially him," Olson said.

Irene Olson, 74, still goes to games. She and 60,789 of her closest friends are the lucky ones. All games are sold out to season-ticket holders, and the waiting list extends from Green Bay to the Golden Gate Bridge.

In 1950, the financially strapped Packers held a

Peggy Hill and Bill Croy of Ashwaubenon tied the knot prior to a Packers game this season.

stock drive that raised $118,000. The community dollars kept the team from folding.

And in 1957, the new City Stadium (renamed Lambeau Field when Lambeau died in 1965) was built in a corn field in the southwest corner of Green Bay.

Homes popped up around it, and it was as if Lambeau Field had become a neighborhood park.

Doug VandeVoort, a retired ironworker, helped on the construction of the Packers' new home before building his own on Stadium Drive. The east-west bordering street put him close enough to hear Vince Lombardi holler at the players, he said.

With these two events — allowing the team to become community-owned and building the new stadium — the Packers cemented their commitment to call Green Bay "home."

Today, fans continue to embrace the Packers as family.

Football fans in Green Bay thought of little other

The Packers put the chill on their opponents in 1996 — they were 10-0 at Lambeau, including two playoff games.

than the Packers during the 1960's. Who could blame them? The Pro Football Hall of Fame was in their back yards. Bart Starr. Jerry Kramer. Willie Wood. Ray Nitschke. Forrest Gregg. Paul Hornung. And, of course, Vince Lombardi.

Lombardi's philosophies set well in this blue-collar city. The legendary coach also inspired a new legion of Packers fans, with fan clubs worldwide.

Laurie Hayes, a Packers fan from Mosman Park, Australia, attended this season's Monday Night Football game against the San Francisco 49ers. The 50-year-old technical school teacher became a fan 30-some years ago after falling under Lombardi's spell a half a world away.

"All Muslims go to Mecca once in their lifetime; I just had to go to Green Bay," she said.

Lambeau Field is holy ground to Packer fans. There is a pure, non-commercial aura about the stadium, with its modest seating and limited skyboxes. It's a stadium where the grass playing field takes its rightful top billing, even gaining its own mystique: the frozen tundra.

As Monday Night Football commentator Dan Dierdorf said earlier this season, "I grew up worshipping the game of professional football and the Packers and Lambeau Field. I don't want to sound corny, but those are images from my youth that are just crystal clear. They're solid as a rock."

Local fans even choose to celebrate one of life's most important events at Lambeau.

Bill Croy and Peggy Hill of Ashwaubenon, the village southwest of Green Bay, got married a few hours before the kickoff of this season's Monday night game between the Packers and the Philadelphia Eagles.

"We have a great time here," Hill said. "And I think of Lambeau Field as our Sunday church."

Packers fans were patient during the team's uninspired play during the 1970's and 80's. They watched

the coaches come and go.

And they waited.

Mind you, the Packers were still a way of life in Green Bay. Teachers like Andrea Knutson of MacArthur Elementary School were using the Packers' road schedule to teach geography to her students long before this dream season of 1996. And folks have

Green Bay | GOTTA LOVE THE PACK

Fans waited 29 years for another Super Bowl champ. Vince Lombardi delivered the last title, after the 1967 season.

always avoided scheduling meetings, church activities and special events on a game day, unless they wanted dismal attendance.

But when the team got off to a roaring start this season, Green Bay fans got on the edge of their seats.

Packer-mania reached a new level.

Indeed, Lambeau rocked with cheers reaching 100-plus decibels (140 or higher causes pain) during the Packers-49ers Monday night game. A reporter from The Press-Gazette recorded it, using a portable sound

Lambeau Field is heaven on Earth to thousands of fans who finally saw their Packers win another Super Bowl.

level meter.

The highest reading? When Chris Jacke kicked a field goal in overtime, giving the Packers a 23-20 victory.

Those two-legged animals known as tailgaters also sensed that something special was brewing this season. The smoke from their grills hung on the stadium's shoulders before each home game. Rain or shine.

Harold Froehlich of Appleton was among those who fought the rain and the cold of the Jan. 4 divisional playoff game against San Francisco.

"This is the important part because we get revved up for the game," he said as rain slid off his shoulders.

The zaniness increased as the regular season drew to a close.

The "Packarena" — the Green Bay fans' version of the popular Spanish club song Macarena — made its way into the stands and onto the streets just in time for the Packers' 41-6 dance over the Denver Broncos in December.

At the second Green Bay-Minnesota meeting in December, the last game of the regular season, two friends were dressed as Christmas trees, trimmed with Vikings and Packers footballs, key chains and other ornaments.

Even Santa Claus showed his true colors at Marie Osmond's touring Christmas show in December — they weren't green and red, but rather, green and gold.

Santa, to the delight of the audience, said he would deliver the Vince Lombardi Trophy to Green Bay.

The home-field advantage the Packers earned for the playoffs was an early Christmas gift to the fans. Season-ticket holders happily mailed in checks for playoff tickets.

A transplanted Carolina couple tried to describe to how they became Packers fans after moving here and following the Panthers their first season.

It was the fans and it was the air, they said. In this town there is definitely a Green Bay Packers' air and

Green Bay | GOTTA LOVE THE PACK

Bev and Bob Berken of DePere admire a snowman constructed in honor of Packers defensive end Reggie White.

you can't help but breathe it in.

Sandy Hoffman and her brother, Tim, played in the snow outside Sandy's Green Bay home on New Year's Day with Sandy's daughter, Anna.

They didn't make a snowman. They didn't make snow angels.

They built an enormous Packers helmet.

What fans had been waiting 29 years for finally happened in January, when Lawrence Luther shivered with the thousands of other fans at Lambeau, both inside and out.

The Packers spanked the Carolina Panthers, 30-13, claiming the NFC championship title and the right to play the New England Patriots in Super Bowl XXXI in New Orleans.

The crowd remained at Lambeau for a long, long time after the clock ran out. The players did, too.

It was a family celebration.

As Pro Bowl defensive lineman Reggie White said after taking a victory lap around the stadium: "Green Bay, I hope you're proud of us, because we're proud of you."

Packers	10	14	10	0	34
Bucanneers	0	3	0	0	3

Packers Hit Jackpot

BY PETE DOUGHERTY
Press-Gazette

TAMPA, SEPT. 1, 1996 — This must have been what Ron Wolf and Mike Holmgren envisioned when they re-signed Keith Jackson in July.

It's a move many teams wouldn't have made, investing $3 million a year in the tight end position for two Pro Bowl-caliber players: Jackson and Mark Chmura.

But General Manager Wolf and Coach Holmgren had seen at the end of last season what a lethal combination those players could be in Holmgren's diverse passing offense.

And on Sunday, the players picked up right where they left off in a 34-3 win over Tampa Bay.

After a full training camp together, Jackson and Chmura combined for 100 yards receiving Sunday, and Jackson had three first-half touchdown catches. The last Packer to catch three TD's in one game was Sterling Sharpe in 1994.

"That's got to be the best tandem in the league," Tampa Bay cornerback Martin Mayhew said. "A lot of teams would have said, 'We have Chmura, so let's let Jackson go.' They didn't, and it's paying dividends."

The Packers didn't realize what they had with Chmura when they traded for Jackson last season, but he built the foundation for a Pro Bowl season while Jackson held out for 91 days. Then, once Jackson got into decent physical shape late in the year, they showed glimpses of what a potent duo they could be. In the last eight games, including three playoff games and Sunday's opener, they have combined for 46 receptions for 698 yards and 10 touchdowns.

"That's why they signed both of us," Chmura said. "We really are one guy in a sense."

Against the Buccaneers, Chmura and Jackson not only substituted for each other regularly, they also played together frequently. The Packers had three straight scoring possessions in the second and third quarters where they played primarily with one running back, and on many of those they chose to go with Jackson and Chmura instead of a three- or four-receiver set.

In less than seven minutes of game time, the Packers scored on touchdown passes of 4 yards and 51 yards to Jackson, and on a 40-yard field goal by Chris Jacke that gave them a 27-3 lead with just less than 10 minutes left in the third quarter.

Receiver Don Beebe likens the Packers' attack to the one during his seven years with Buffalo that included four straight Super Bowl appearances. The Bills, for part of that time, had a diverse corps of weapons with receivers Andre Reed, James Lofton and Beebe, and running back Thurman Thomas, a top-notch runner and receiver.

The Bills then turned up the pressure on defenses by running a no-huddle attack. The Packers, with Jackson and Chmura, can bombard teams in a different way, similar to a baseball pitcher who has command of several pitches.

Packers tight end Keith Jackson celebrates the first of his three touchdowns against Tampa Bay in the season opener.

Quicker Defense Gets Six Turnovers

BY CHRIS HAVEL
Press-Gazette

A Packers defense that struggled to force turnovers last season thrived on Sunday with a new lineup and a new attitude. The changes included Santana Dotson at tackle, Brian Williams at linebacker and Eugene Robinson at free safety.

The result: speed kills.

The Packers forced the Buccaneers into six turnovers while dominating first-year Coach Tony Dungy's team, 34-3.

Packers defensive end Sean Jones was asked to describe the difference in the defense's overall speed from last season to this season.

"Night and day," he said.

Jones said there were several plays in which he thought the Bucs were going to make good yardage, only to see the running back or receiver leveled for minimal gains.

"One play I turned it in and I'm saying, 'Where's my force? Where's my force?' and Brian Williams comes flying in to make the tackle for a 6-yard loss," Jones said. "Team speed is like bat speed in baseball. Once you have it, it doesn't mean you'll hit a home run all the time, but your chances are better."

Defensive coordinator Fritz Shurmur said the new linebacking corps of Williams, Wayne Simmons and George Koonce has dramatically increased the defense's speed.

"There's no question that the three linebackers, plus Santana Dotson and Eugene Robinson, makes us a lot faster," he said. "It shows in terms of running to the ball and making plays against the passing game. That's where it shows. You've got to defend the whole field and to do that, you've got to have guys with speed."

The Bucs were limited to 176 total yards of offense. More important, they were a dismal 2 of 10 on third-down conversions. Tampa Bay's only third-down conversion against the Packers' dime package (six defensive backs) came on its third play from scrimmage, a 7-yard completion to receiver Courtney Hawkins.

Shurmur used rookie Tyrone Williams at right corner and veteran Mike Prior at safety, along with starters Craig Newsome (left corner), Doug Evans (who moved to the slot), LeRoy Butler (who played near the line) and safety Robinson.

Simmons stayed on the field as the lone dime linebacker, while Shurmur rotated rookie Keith McKenzie, tackle Darius Holland and end Gabe Wilkins in the front four. The Buccaneers had little running room all day, managing just 59 yards on 23 carries.

Bucs quarterback Trent Dilfer cited the Packers' defensive line, led by Reggie White, Jones and ex-Buccaneer Dotson, as a major reason for the lopsided outcome.

When asked about the six turnovers, Dilfer said, "When you go up against that front four, you've got your hands full."

Asked about the lack of a running game, he said, "There just weren't a lot of holes."

Shurmur acknowledged the Packers got some good bounces, but he said the defense's hard hitting could not be overlooked.

"It was a big deal that we came up with the ball, but part of it was because we hit extremely well after the catch," he said. "When it was fumbled, we were on it."

Craig Newsome and the Packers defense forced the Bucs into six turnovers and limited their offense to 176 total yards.

"You always have to be on your toes because we substitute guys every play," Beebe said. "Very rarely will we call the same formation or have the same guys on the field for two plays in a row."

On Sunday, Jackson had a big day because the Buccaneers slanted their pass coverages toward receiver Robert Brooks. Brooks caught three passes for only 25 yards.

That helped Jackson spring wide open on several plays on his way to five receptions for 76 yards. The biggest was the 51-yarder late in the first half, when quarterback Brett Favre stepped up in the pocket to avoid the rush, giving Jackson time to break free down the middle of the field. It was the kind of play Jackson's speed allowed him to deliver last year in the playoffs.

"(Jackson) certainly makes us a better team," Wolf said. "He's a great player, and when you add a great player to your arsenal, it allows you to do so many things."

Wolf mentioned Holmgren's offense, which he learned from former 49ers coach Bill Walsh, as ideal for utilizing tight ends. Then he pointed to Favre, who was being interviewed about 10 feet away after a nearly flawless day of 20 of 27 passing for 247 yards and four touchdowns.

"That guy there helps out a lot, too," he said.

Packers	10	20	7	2	39
Eagles	0	7	0	6	13

Prime Time Pounding

By Pete Dougherty
Press-Gazette

GREEN BAY, SEPT. 9, 1996 — Brett Favre opened Monday night's show-down with the Philadelphia Eagles by misfiring on his first five passes and taking the Packers a total of 9 yards the first three times they had the ball.

They had run so few plays that by their fourth possession they still were on Coach Mike Holmgren's first-15-plays script. Next on the list was a call that's been Holmgren's most reliable since bringing his version of the San Francisco 49ers' offense to Green Bay in 1992 – a screen pass.

Favre goaded the Eagles' heavy rush, then dumped the ball to halfback Edgar Bennett, who picked up 11 yards and a first down. As unremarkable as it appeared at the time, it opened the floodgates of an offensive explosion. The Packers' remarkably diverse offense embarrassed the Eagles, 39-13, in front of a Monday night, national TV audience and a jubilant record crowd of 60,666 at Lambeau.

After the game, Holmgren characterized his script's screen call as "timely."

"Sometimes it's just a matter of throwing a screen pass, getting a completion or calming things down a bit," he said. "I think that's what happened."

The Packers are 2-0 with a combined scoring differential of 73-16.

The startling part of the blowout was the quality of opponent. If last week's season-opening 34-3 hammering of Tampa Bay could be written off as catching a weak team in its first game with a new coach, Monday night, by all appearances, was to present a real challenge.

The Eagles came in as one of the NFL's teams on the rise and regarded as a contender for the NFC Eastern Division title.

They also had a coach, Ray Rhodes, who has a reputation as a master motivator, not to mention an intimate knowledge of the Packers after serving as Holmgren's defensive coordinator in 1992 and '93.

But the game was over by halftime, when Green Bay led, 30-7, and the Packers are sure to open eyes around the NFL. After Monday night, the question that has dogged the Packers for the past three years — whether they've closed the gap on Dallas and San Francisco — seems to have disappeared.

"What I saw tonight was a team that realized it can be a great team," said Sean Jones, a Packers defensive end.

And it all started with the screen pass to Bennett.

Holmgren has leaned heavily on that play in his five years as Packers coach, especially when his offense was less talented than now, and often when it was struggling to move the ball.

It's become such an effective weapon that last season Chicago Bears coach Dave Wannstedt showed his

Dorsey Levens helped the Packers rush for 171 yards against the Eagles, who only gained 59 on the ground.

team an entire videotape of Packers screens the week before their second meeting.

Bennett still managed to score on screens of 17 and 16 yards that day, and on Monday night he scored in similar fashion. Besides getting that first catch, he also put on the finishing touch on the win in the third quarter, taking a screen pass 25 yards for the Packers' final touchdown and a 37-7 lead.

"It's something we practice and Mike harps on more than anything in this offense," tight end Mark Chmura said. "You don't see many teams run it in the red zone, and we run it down there real well. We pride ourselves on it."

The first completion probably did more than just get Favre started. It might have taken the edge off pass-rushing defensive ends William Fuller and Mike Mamula.

After that 11-yard screen, Favre completed 13 of his next 20 passes while taking the Packers to five straight scores — three touchdowns and two field goals

This One Was Over Shortly After Coin Toss

BY CHRIS HAVEL
Press-Gazette

You could sift through the wreckage for clues as to why the Packers annihilated the Eagles. Or you could merely listen to noted philosopher/nose tackle Gilbert Brown.

"Ain't no secrets. Ain't no tricks," he said. "We just played good football."

Brown, a big man of few words, was correct in both his analysis of the Packers' 39-13 shelling of Philadelphia and his decision not to overstate the obvious.

Simply put, the Packers are one of the NFL's top teams. The Eagles are not. That debate started to die in the split-second between Chris T. Jones' catch and Doug Evans' interception, all of which happened on the Eagles' first play.

Evans' sleight of hand not only set the tone, but also the tint, the hue and the color of the Packers' first home appearance on Monday Night Football in a decade. This game was green and gold and red (with the Eagles' embarrassment) all over.

The Packers are unbeaten. They are better than they were last season, when they were very good. The Packers have given all their critics little to nit-pick.

OK. So Eugene Robinson misplayed the catch-and-lateral. And George Koonce and Sean Jones dropped would-be interceptions. And Mike Arthur's snap sailed higher than Hakeem Olajuwon can reach with a golf ball retriever.

In the past, those would've made headlines. Today, they're footnotes.

The Packers have won 19 of their last 20 at Lambeau Field, a feat unmatched even by Lombardi's teams. This is a franchise whose present has finally outrun its past, fueled by a team whose future seems limitless.

The Packers came in as 8-point favorites for a reason. The reason is no one in their right mind would bet on the Eagles unless they were getting two scores before the pregame introductions. The Packers are hot. Or as an acquaintance noted, "If this were college football, the Packers would be No.1."

By that logic, if this were college football, the Packers would be host to the TCU Horned Frogs instead of the San Diego Chargers this weekend. Of course, the Horned Frogs are not the Chargers, but then the Eagles weren't the Eagles. They were the Buccaneers in midnight green.

The Packers took the zip out of the Eagles by forcing three turnovers on their first four possessions. Asked if his presence as honorary game captain affected the outcome, ex-Packers center Larry McCarren laughed and said, "Oh, I figure that and Ed West losing the coin toss pretty much sealed it."

Yep. This one was over early.

In the span of two quarters, the Packers cut the Eagles in half, reducing a Super Bowl XXXI contender to a .500 team with a quarterback controversy.

This is how tough it was on the Eagles: Their only break come on the bad snap that caused the Packers to botch a field-goal try. Their reward was the ball at their own 3-yard line. That series ended with Reggie White and Santana Dotson sacking Rodney Peete for a safety.

Talk about costly turnovers. Ty Detmer once more was the second-best quarterback at Lambeau Field, right behind Brett Favre but well ahead of Peete.

— before the half ended.

"With the pursuit they were bringing, the way to slow it down is with draws and screens," Favre said.

Then the Packers' offensive diversity overwhelmed the Eagles.

Last week, the killers were tight ends Keith Jackson and Chmura, who against Tampa Bay combined for 100 yards receiving and Jackson's three touchdowns.

This week, the Eagles kept Jackson and Chmura from getting behind the secondary and limited them to four receptions for 58 yards.

But when Philadelphia's big cornerbacks, Bobby Taylor (6-foot-3, 216 pounds) and Troy Vincent (6-0, 194), tried to jam receivers Robert Brooks and Antonio Freeman at the line of scrimmage, they had little help from the safeties. The price was devastating.

Brooks gashed them for 130 yards on five receptions, a 26-yard average.

After catching a 25-yard pass for the Packers' first touchdown, he streaked straight past tight one-on-one coverage for three big plays on perfect throws from Favre — 38-yarder behind Vincent that set up a touchdown; a 33-yarder behind safety Eric Zomalt that set up a field goal; and a 20-yarder behind Vincent for the final first-half touchdown.

With weapons such as Brooks, Freeman, Chmura, Jackson and Bennett, Holmgren kept the Eagles off balance with a variety of formations — two tight ends on some plays, three or four receivers on others, and the standard two-back set on others. Once Favre got started the Packers dominated, finishing with 432 total yards, averaging 15.4 yards a completion, and rushing for more yards (171) than any game last season.

"This guy right here," said Jones, pointing at Favre's locker, "just does some things that aren't coached. It's God-given. That ball he threw to Brooks on the second (20-yard) touchdown — that ball was on a line, on the money, effortless. That kind of confidence,

Mike Johnson punishes quarterback Ty Detmer of the Eagles, who were limited to 259 yards total offense.

where does it come from?"

Two weeks into the season, that confidence has filtered through this team. The Packers' back-to-back dominating wins are sure to make them the talk of the NFL.

"It doesn't matter what they're saying," Favre said. "It's what we're thinking."

Packers	7	14	7	14	42
Chargers	3	0	0	7	10

Front Four Dominates

By Pete Dougherty
Press-Gazette

GREEN BAY, SEPT. 15, 1996 — And so it goes, as it has for three weeks with the Green Bay Packers' defense:

It holds an opponent to fewer than two touchdowns, and two defensive linemen have big games — in this case, ends Sean Jones and Reggie White with two sacks each.

Then tackle Santana Dotson draws a huge postgame crowd of reporters because as a key new player this year he surely must be a reason why the Packers are limiting opponents to 192 yards a game.

And then there's Gilbert Brown. The stat sheet after the Packers' 42-10 blowout of San Diego on Sunday says he had one assisted tackle for the day, and nothing more. But that can't begin to measure what this massive, 350-pound tackle brings to the heart of this defense.

"Gilbert gets all the dirty work," Jones said. "We let Gilbert sit in there and pick up all the trash and Reggie and I get to slash and go. That's his fault for being so good. Without a guy like that (for the offense) to respect ... that's what makes everything go."

For a third straight week the Packers' defense was as dominating as their offense — their average margin of victory in their 3-0 start is 38-9.

And it all starts with the defensive line of Jones, White, Dotson and Brown.

White, at age 34, still is the key and remains one of the most dominating players in the game. He had several pressures to go with his two sacks, one of which caused a fumble the Chargers recovered.

"(The Packers) took Reggie White as a cornerstone, like a Michael Jordan, and added guys around him," linebacker George Koonce said.

Brown, a fourth-year pro, quietly has become as valued a piece as any of his highly paid linemates, who are under contract for a combined average salary of $8.4 million a year.

Facing an offensive line that Bobby Ross calls his best in five years as the Chargers' coach, the Packers shut down a San Diego rushing game that was averaging 100 yards with three very different runners splitting time in its one-back attack: 240-pound Leonard Russell, 218-pound Aaron Hayden and 196-pound Terrell Fletcher.

The Packers limited them to a combined 33 yards and a 2.5-yard average per carry. Brown is not the only reason, but he is their primary run stopper in the

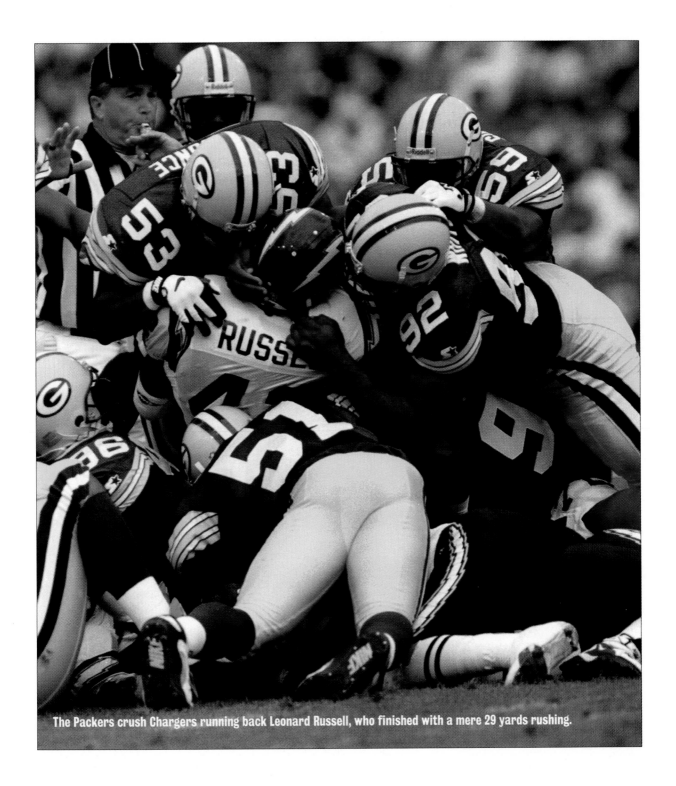

The Packers crush Chargers running back Leonard Russell, who finished with a mere 29 yards rushing.

Game 3 | PACKERS 42, CHARGERS 10

middle of the field.

With that under control, the Packers besieged quarterback Stan Humphries. Besides sacking him four times, they had several other hard hits and had him scrambling most of the day. He finished with barely over a 50 percent completion percentage (16-for-30) and only 130 yards passing.

As they have all year, the Chargers generally kept in a tight end on pass plays, which gave them six blockers against four linemen and an occasional blitz from linebacker Wayne Simmons or safety LeRoy Butler. But which two should they have double-teamed?

"(Most weeks) you consider which guy is the pass-rush specialist and you try to eliminate him," Humphries said. "It's kind of hard to do when you've got four guys up there."

Brown, the only Packers starter on the defensive line who doesn't have a sack this season, drew as many double teams as anyone.

"Big Gil, you have to get him double teamed or some offensive lineman is going to get pushed into the quarterback for sure," Koonce said.

Dotson also has been a huge factor since the Pack-

ers signed him in the offseason for an average of $2 million a year to replace John Jurkovic.

The Packers have allowed an unusually low completion percentage so far (46.5 percent), and that's where the pass rush is crucial. Fritz Shurmur, their defensive coordinator, said he's blitzed a little more this year than last, but Dotson's rushing speed from the middle of the line has been a bigger factor as more teams go to short quarterback drops.

"In the 80's you had the small linebacker types that you called defensive ends (as the key pass rushers)," Shurmur said. "Now you have to get somebody in (the quarterback's) face quick. That's the way the game has changed, and (Dotson) has been a factor in there."

The Packers started well early last season also, limiting the Rams and Giants to 17 points or less in two of the first three games before hard times hit in the middle of the year. But even in those early early games they were giving up much more yardage than now. The Rams and Bears both gained more than 300 yards against Green Bay in the first three games of '95.

The differences this year, other than Dotson, have been moving Koonce to middle linebacker, supplanting Fred Strickland; replacing Koonce at right outside linebacker with second-year pro Brian Williams; signing Eugene Robinson to replace George Teague at strong safety; and playing Butler as a cover man and blitzer in the middle of the field on many passing downs.

The only mistakes of consequence the Packers' defense made were two penalties that converted third downs for San Diego. They led to 10 points: A roughing penalty when Williams hit Humphries with a forearm to the head on a blitz, and an interference on rookie cornerback Tyrone Williams.

Santana Dotson and the Packers limited the Chargers to just 11 first downs and 141 yards of total offense.

Old Super Bowl Champs Ready To Pass Torch

BY JOHN MORTON
Press-Gazette

On Sunday evening in Green Bay, many people were talking about not only one Super Bowl, but two.

They weren't greedy fans of the Packers' current team. They were the members of the Packers' two-time Super Bowl champions of yesteryear.

The list of Packers alumni introduced at the Regency Conference Center Sunday read much like the famed Packers sweep itself: Bowman, Kramer, Thurston, followed by Anderson, Mercein and Grabowski.

On the defensive side were legendary Packers such as Ray Nitschke, Herb Adderly and Willie Wood.

They gathered with members of the community to benefit the local Boys & Girls Club and to celebrate the Packers' Super Bowl championship teams of 1967 and '68. Each player, when introduced, was escorted by a child from the club.

As the legendary Packers walked through the audience, a spotlight followed them to their tables. But these days, they know the spotlight has spread to the current team as well. "It's about time," former Packers guard Fuzzy Thurston said. "It's been way, way too long."

"It's one of the reasons why we're here," added Dave Robinson, a standout linebacker on those title teams. "We want the guys to know there's not just an old Green Bay Packers, but one Green Bay Packers."

More than 20 players from Super Bowls I and II attended the event. During the day, they watched from the sidelines as the current Packers destroyed San Diego. Just like those Vince Lombardi teams did so often.

"It seems like yesterday when we were here, win-

Ray Nitschke shows his Super Bowl ring to Russ and Julie Anhalt of Cato at the Boys & Girls Club function.

ning those championships," Robinson said.

The old Packers talked about the past, but they are glad there's a bright future. "At first we didn't want someone to take our spot," said Super Bowl I and II guard Jerry Kramer, "but then we got impatient. Now, we're more than happy to pass the torch."

Vikings	7	7	3	13	30
Packers	7	0	14	0	21

Vikes Frustrate Packers

By Pete Dougherty
Press-Gazette

Minneapolis, Sept. 22, 1996 — Without time to throw, the NFL's hottest quarterback and reigning MVP might as well have been an undrafted rookie on Sunday.

Brett Favre was on an incredible streak coming into Sunday's meeting of the NFC Central Division's two undefeated teams, having thrown 37 touchdown passes and only five interceptions in his previous 13 games, including last year's playoffs.

But the Vikings reduced him to a shell of that player by putting him under siege from start to finish in a 30-21 win over the Packers at the Metrodome. They did it by dominating the Packers' offensive line, both man-for-man and with an array of blitzes that had Favre dodging, ducking and twisting in and out of the pocket the majority of times he went back to pass.

After three weeks in which he had been knocked down infrequently and sacked but three times, Favre on Sunday took one of the toughest beatings of his NFL career and was sacked seven times.

"We didn't play worth a (crap)," center Frank Winters said of the offensive line. "That's kind of harsh, but it's true. (Favre) got hit a lot."

The win gives the Vikings the early lead in the NFC Central with a 4-0 record, a game ahead of the 3-1 Packers.

The seven sacks were the most the Packers have allowed in Mike Holmgren's five seasons as head coach,

and that more than fairly represents what a bad day the offensive line had.

The most obvious struggles belonged to left tackle Gary Brown, who in the first three games this year as Ken Ruetggers' replacement appeared as though he was on his way to securing the starting job for the rest of the season. But by the end of the first half Sunday, he had been beaten by three different Vikings — tackle John Randle, and defensive ends Derrick Alexander and Martin Harrison.

Brown, a third-year pro, didn't get overpowered, but simply was unable to match the Vikings' speed on the outside of their defensive line. Randle beat him around the end for the first sack, on third down, late in the first quarter, and the Vikings threw a heavy dose of fastballs at him thereafter that were enhanced by the crowd noise at the Metrodome. It was difficult for both teams to hear snap counts and audibles.

Harrison, who is Alexander's backup, is a speed rusher who is about as light a defensive end comes at 251 pounds. He finished with two sacks.

"It's like a hitter (in baseball). You go up there and strike out three times and it gets tough," said Tom Lovat, the Packers' offensive line coach. "Sometimes

Vikings defensive end Martin Harrison escorts Packers quarterback Brett Favre to his seat in the Metrodome.

when a guy has your number ... (Brown) had his ups and downs, that's for sure."

Brown struggled enough that Lovat considered replacing him with rookie John Michels. Michels is getting close to regaining full-strength from a sprained ankle he suffered in the third week of the exhibition season, an injury that cost him the starting job up to now because Brown had played well in his place.

"Pretty close," Lovat said when asked how close he came to putting in Michels. "But we felt like we could help Gary out, and he was lathered up, so we decided to bite the bullet and go."

This was the first time in the regular season the Packers have truly missed having Ruettgers, who is on the physically-unable-to-perform list. After the sixth game the Packers will have three weeks to activate him, and his degenerative left knee has improved enough in the past month that his return remains a possibility.

For the more immediate future, Lovat said he at least will consider starting Michels this week against Seattle.

For his part, Brown offered no excuse: "All I know is, I had a bad day."

The pressure came from other angles as well — Randle and Harrison had two sacks each, and Alexander, left end Fernando Smith and cornerback Alfred Jackson had one each. That made it tough on Favre and the Packers' offense, which had appeared unstoppable in the first three games this year.

It came into Sunday leading the NFL in scoring (38.3 points a game), total yards (395.6 a game) and third-down efficiency (a 55.8 percent conversion rate).

The Vikings destroyed all that. They limited the Packers to 217 yards and a 1-for-11 conversion rate on third downs. The Packers' offense in effect consisted of one big play — receiver Don Beebe's 80-yard touchdown reception — along with four turnovers

and seven drive-killing penalties.

Favre fumbled on three different sacks, and the Vikings recovered two of them, one of which set them up on the Packers' 4 for an eventual touchdown.

The penalties were costly also, most especially one late in the second quarter, when Favre hit Robert Brooks wide open crossing over the middle. Brooks turned the play into a 60-yard gain to the Vikings' 14 that put the Packers in position to immediately answer a Minnesota touchdown that had put the Vikings ahead, 14-7. But Brown was penalized for holding.

Winters was called for holding two plays later, nullifying fullback William Henderson's 15-yard run, and the Packers never did get a first down before punting.

Both Brown and Winters were penalized on an earlier drive that ended with a punt also — Brown for tripping and Winters for a 15-yard personal foul.

"They're quick off the ball," Winters said of the

Packers Trip On Familiar Bump

BY CHRIS HAVEL
Press-Gazette

After needing three weeks to showcase their numerous strengths, the Packers required only three hours to reveal their various weaknesses.

Proportionally, that sounds about right, though it's likely Packers coach Mike Holmgren would rather his team unveil its shortcomings in less convincing fashion.

"Too many turnovers. Too many penalties," Holmgren said. "That's unacceptable."

Undeniable, too.

The Packers' 30-21 loss to the Vikings proves beyond a doubt they are not perfect. Neither are the Vikings,

but at 4-0, at least they've got the record to spark a logical debate. They've also got the lead in the NFC Central, a proposition that seemed farfetched a day ago.

"We step on our own feet here," Packers quarterback Brett Favre said about the Metrodome. "I don't think it's so much what Minnesota does, but what we do."

What the Packers do here is lose with dazzling regularity. Their string of Metrodome disasters is at five and counting. The Packers' performance here, as usual, had its share of folly, the majority of which occurred at left tackle.

To say Gary Brown struggled would be like saying the Titanic sprung a leak. Brown made anyone fortunate enough to line up across from him look like the

Game 4 | SEPTEMBER 22, 1996

Vikings. "We've been playing here for five years and it's the same thing. You can attribute it to the noise — I don't know. It's like deja vu. It's kind of hard to talk about, you get so frustrated."

Despite the struggles, the Packers still had a chance to win in the fourth quarter. Twice they had the ball in the last 4 minutes 13 seconds with a chance to take the lead but couldn't get a first down, let alone a touchdown.

On those two potential go-ahead drives, the Vikings' pass rush was the difference. Randle sacked Favre on the first play of the first one, causing a fumble that Alexander recovered. On the second, Esera Tuoalo and Randle sacked Favre for a 4-yard loss on first down. And when the Packers went for it on fourth-and-8, the Vikings nearly got Favre again and forced him into a hurried incompletion on a pass to a covered Mark Chmura.

That left the Packers without a win in their last five trips to the Metrodome.

The Packers' Don Beebe scoots his way to an 80-yard touchdown reception during the third quarter.

second coming of Chris Doleman, though Chris Farley might have done the trick the way he played.

During the game, Packers GM Ron Wolf yelled, "Hey, protect the quarterback!" His comment was directed at the officials, though the Packers' offensive line would've been the better target.

After the game, Holmgren was asked if he thought about putting in John Michels, to which he replied, "No."

Hopefully, that was "no" as in, "No, because I chose to stick with Gary Brown," rather than "No, it never occurred to me." Because it sure as heck occurred to everyone else.

Holmgren said he wanted to see the film before he would speak of this team's pass protection. That really wasn't necessary because, film or no film, there was no protection to speak of.

Favre was sacked seven times, hurried 15 times and knocked down eight times. Those numbers explain these: 14-of-27 for 198 yards and an interception. He managed two touchdown passes, but they were the result of Eugene Robinson's interception and Don Beebe's speed.

The Packers' offensive was ineffective. It converted 1-of-11 third downs. It managed just eight first downs. It committed four turnovers.

The Vikings' Robert Smith rushed for more yards on a single play (37) than Edgar Bennett mustered all afternoon (33).

To the Packers' credit, they stood behind Brown, a risky proposition on this day.

"Only a blind man would make Gary Brown the scapegoat," defensive end Sean Jones said.

The Packers reacted to defeat with defiance. Theirs is the attitude of a champion. They appear to be a team that has no intention of making this a habit.

| Packers | 10 | 7 | 7 | 7 | 31 |
| Seahawks | 0 | 7 | 3 | 0 | 10 |

Defense Steals One

By Pete Dougherty
Press-Gazette

SEATTLE, SEPT. 29, 1996 — If the Packers' amazing turnover turnaround has several explanations, Eugene Robinson has to head the list.

The Packers' new starting free safety is the NFL's interception leader among active players with 44 in his 12-year career. Since being traded to the Packers during the summer, he's helped his new team improve in that regard. They've gone from 13 interceptions last season, tied for fourth-worst in the NFL, to a league-leading 15 only five games into 1996.

Four of those picks came Sunday in the Packers' 31-10 win over Seattle. It was Robinson's homecoming — he played his first 11 seasons for the Seahawks — and the five turnovers the Packers forced gave them the commanding win on a day when their offensive struggles could have made for a much tighter game.

"He's brought us a consciousness of catching the ball," said safety LeRoy Butler, who has four interceptions this season but had none Sunday. "I don't think we've dropped any (potential interceptions) yet."

The turnovers Sunday were important because they set up quarterback Brett Favre in Seattle territory for

The Packers' Sean Jones halts Seahawks quarterback John Friesz on fourth down.

Game 5 | PACKERS 31, SEAHAWKS 10

the game's first three scores after the offense had no first downs and no points in its first three possessions.

Robinson had the first takeaway when Seattle receiver Brian Blades was cut off on a double move and quarterback Rick Mirer tried to throw the ball away with a long lob pass inside the Packers' 10. Robinson's 39-yard return set up a touchdown.

End Reggie White's interception on the Seahawks' next possession set up a 36-yard field goal by Chris Jacke, and linebacker Wayne Simmons forced a Mirer fumble on a sack near the end of the first half that set up another TD and gave the Packers a 17-0 lead.

Even though Robinson's interception give him two for the season, his impact hasn't been his own production in games as much as his influence in practice.

The most obvious change he's brought is in inter-

ception drills. Since the start of training camp, the Packers defensive backs have been using two new drills. Both were drills Robinson learned in Seattle.

The first is a drill with the "Jugs" throwing machine. It's set at the high end of an NFL quarterback's throwing speed, and the players stand anywhere from 15 yards to less than 10 yards from it, trying to make quick-reaction catches.

The other is a catch drill in which the defensive backs are about 15 yards apart. They throw the ball as hard as they can at each other's feet, sometimes with the catcher standing with his back to the ball until it's thrown. The drills are designed to make the catch difficult, and the Packers' extraordinary jump in interceptions suggests they're working.

"You won't be afraid of the ball," Robinson said.

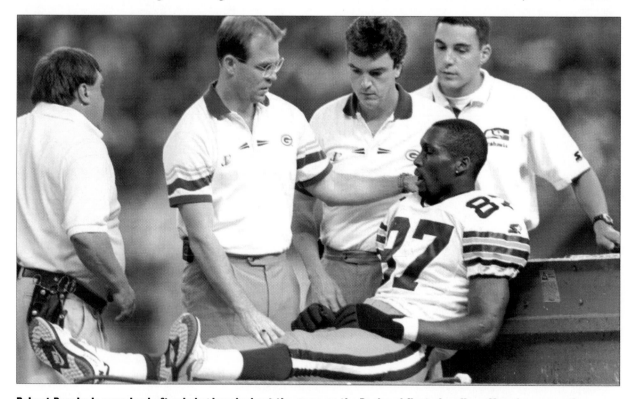

Robert Brooks is examined after being knocked out the game on the Packers' first play. He suffered a concussion.

It Was Like The Packers Never Left Home

BY CHRIS HAVEL
Press-Gazette

For one mostly carefree afternoon Sunday, the Packers overcame their habit of losing road games on turf in a dome. The solution, it seems, it remembering to pack properly.

This time, unlike a week ago at Minnesota, the Packers brought a killer defense, a running attack and lots of pass protection so their quarterback wouldn't sweat onrushing linemen. That and enough fans to inhabit De Pere enabled the Packers to mix business with pleasure in a thorough 31-10 dispatching of the Seahawks.

Safety Eugene Robinson, who played here for 11 seasons, wasn't the only Packer player who felt like it was homecoming. The Kingdome crowd of 59,973 was crawling with Packers fans, discernible by their green jerseys, cheeseheads and chants of "Reg-GIE! Reg-GIE!"

It was only the Packers' second victory in 14 games on the road, on turf, in a dome. So even though it came at the expense of the woeful Seahawks, it was cause for celebration.

"I want that to be the headline of every paper in the country," Packers coach Mike Holmgren said playfully. " 'Holmgren does is on turf.' "

Here's what Holmgren and the Packers did: Improved to 4-1 and regained a share of first in the NFC Central, though this game was more like a weekend getaway than a rugged road trip. Consider the Packers itinerary.

Friday: Hit town. Eat dinner. Relax.

Saturday: Wake up. Go to the Kingdome for a walk-through. Eat dinner. Relax.

Sunday: Wake up. Go to the Kingdome for another walk-through, this time with the Seahawks on the field. Eat them for lunch. Burp up a few feathers. Fly home.

The Packers would've encountered greater resistance trying to get in line for a tour of the Space Needle. Say this for the Seahawks. They play the perfect foil. They made a fight of it for, oh, the first quarter or so before rolling over and playing dead.

By the time Seattle's Chris Warren shrugged a trio of would-be tacklers for a 37-yard TD run, the Packers already led, 17-0. Their only adversity was seeing ace receiver Robert Brooks laid out after a wicked tackle by Seattle's Daryl Williams.

Brooks suffered a concussion, but he'll be OK. Antonio Freeman, his replacement was superb.

"With tragedy comes triumph," tight end Keith Jackson said. "Sometimes Brett (Favre) gets keyed in on Brooks. Today forced him to go to someone else and Freeman stepped up. It goes to show we've got a lot of guys who can play."

Freeman caught a career-high seven passes for 108 yards and two touchdowns.

"Free's a great player," cornerback Doug Evans said. "We didn't miss a beat."

Neither did the Packers' offensive line, which gained a good measure of redemption after last week's debacle in the Metrodome. Favre was sacked twice, but he had enough time to complete 11-of-14 second-half passes for 141 yards and two touchdowns.

Favre now has 16 scoring passes, which puts him on a pace to throw 51 this season. He credited Freeman and the line, in particular rookie left tackle John Michels, who beat out Gary Brown and likely earned a second start at Chicago this week.

Packers	0	20	14	3	37
Bears	0	3	3	0	6

Bad News For Da Bears

By Pete Dougherty
Press-Gazette

Chicago, Oct. 6, 1996 — The Green Bay Packers ultimately regretted not making Robert Brooks a starting receiver in his second NFL season. They have not made the same mistake with Antonio Freeman.

When all signs in training camp this year suggested Freeman was ready for the starting lineup, the Packers didn't hesitate to give him a shot, and six weeks into the season they have developed another bona-fide weapon for their NFL-leading offense.

On Sunday against the Chicago Bears, Freeman had the Packers' biggest receiving day of the season, catching seven passes for 146 yards, including two spectacular touchdown catches that helped the Packers to their fifth blowout victory in six games, 37-6.

Freeman's force feeding is something the Packers wish they would have done with Brooks in his second season, 1993, when they signed aging Mark Clayton for about $900,000. Clayton caught 32 passes that year. Brooks caught 58 the next year as the starter opposite Sterling Sharpe, and this season Freeman is leading the Packers with 27 receptions, which is a pace of 72 for the season.

"When he's out there in the fire, it makes a guy come along," Brooks said. "A guy like Freeman, with the guts he has, you put his back against the wall and he's going to make it happen."

General Manager Ron Wolf said the Packers had targeted Freeman as a player they wanted in the 1995 draft, but mainly as a kick returner and secondarily as a receiver. They took him in the third round, and in little more than a season, he's become just the opposite.

When asked why Freeman wasn't a higher pick, Wolf said, "I honestly don't know the answer to that. He averaged 20 yards a catch (actually 18.2) in college (at Virginia Tech)."

In the last two weeks, Freeman has had his turn as a key element in the Packers' offense. Last week at Seattle, when he became the go-to flanker after Brooks suffered a game-ending concussion on the first play from scrimmage, Freeman had the first 100-yard receiving day of his career. In the last two weeks combined he's caught 14 passes for 254 yards.

On Sunday, the Bears forced the Packers' hand by shading many of their coverages toward Brooks and keeping Green Bay out of its two tight-end alignment by shifting extra cover men to Mark Chmura and Keith Jackson.

The Bears also were vulnerable. Rookie cornerback Walt Harris didn't start because of a toe injury. He was forced into the game when fellow starting cornerback Donnell Woolford suffered a calf injury in the first half that kept him from returning and backup Kevin Miniefield suffered a concussion.

Receiver Robert Brooks hangs onto the ball, despite the jarring hit by Bears safety Mark Carrier.

Linebacker George Koonce (53) and the Packers' defense limited Rashaan Salaam to 43 yards rushing on 20 carries.

That helped make Freeman the best option, and with quarterback Brett Favre playing to near-perfection, the Packers' offense again was dominating. Favre completed 66.7 percent of his passes (18-for-27) for 246 yards, and his four touchdown passes gives him 20 for the season, which has him on pace to break the NFL's single-season record. Miami's Dan Marino holds the record with 48, and at Favre's current rate he will throw 53.

"We have a quarterback who can get the ball to anybody on the field, anywhere on the field," Brooks said.

Favre began working to Freeman late in the first half, connecting on three passes for 42 yards in the Packers' two-minute offense. That set up a 2-yard touchdown pass to Keith Jackson that gave the Packers some breathing room at 14-3.

Freeman's more spectacular plays still were to come, though, and helped the Packers cruise to another easy win.

The first came at the end of the half, after cornerback Doug Evans' interception got Favre the ball back with 20 seconds left.

Coach Mike Holmgren was left to call plays without any help from his assistant coaches in the press box — they had left for the locker room after Jackson's touchdown catch with 35 seconds left. With 11 seconds left and the Packers at midfield, Favre improvised on Holmgren's third-down call, and the Hail Mary pass off a rollout right caught the Bears off-guard.

"Brett told Earl (Dotson, the right tackle), 'I'm coming your way,' so (Dotson) pinned the left end inside, and it worked out," said Tom Lovat, the Packers' offensive line coach.

Favre rolled right, giving three receivers time to get to the end zone. Brooks was deepest, and Freeman took the middle, just over the goal line. As the ball came down Freeman bumped safety Mark Carrier and caught the ball unchallenged as he fell back in the end zone. That gave the Packers two touch-

Packers running back Edgar Bennett goes head-to-head with Bears safety Marty Carter.

downs in the final 35 seconds of the half, and a tight game suddenly became a comfortable 20-3 lead.

"I think everybody else misjudged it, they jumped too early," Brooks said. "(Freeman) was the calm in the storm."

Game 6 | PACKERS 37, BEARS 6

Packers running back Travis Jervey darts between Bears linebacker Barry Minter and cornerback James Burton (35).

If Freeman's other spectacular catch lacked the shock value that the Hail Mary had on the last play of a half, it actually was the more difficult of the two. It came in the third quarter, when he was matched up one-on-one with Miniefield at the Bears' 35.

The Packers' offensive line gave Favre the time to wait out Freeman's double move, and Freeman did the rest. Favre underthrew his lob to the front corner of the end zone, but Freeman slowed and made the catch by diving over the 5-foot-9 Miniefield.

"At about the 10, I snuck a peak back and saw (the ball) dropping and it was short," Freeman said. "I was able to go up and make the grab."

Both catches reminded Jackson of a former teammate in Philadelphia, Fred Barnett, who is one of the best receivers in the NFL at catching the ball in a crowd.

"That was an outstanding catch," Jackson said of Freeman's second touchdown. "Our quarterback coach (Marty Mornhinweg) tells Brett all the time, 'If it's even (between the receiver and the defensive back), throw the ball up and the receiver will make the play.' "

Freeman's second touchdown put the Packers over the 30-point mark for the fifth time this season, and their 34-6 lead ensured another rout of the Bears. The Packers have averaged 34.4 points in beating Chicago five straight games

Message Comes Through Loud And Clear

BY CHRIS HAVEL
Press-Gazette

When you cut through all the highfalutin' terminology, the Packers' game plan for the Chicago Bears, and anyone else who crosses their path, can be summed up in a word.

Domination.

That has been Coach Mike Holmgren's mission statement since the start of training camp. It might not be as provocative as "Seek and Destroy" or "Divide and Conquer" but it is effective. Through six games, the Packers' margin of victory has come in two sizes: Gilbert and Brown.

"When Mike gets us together, he tells us, 'When people think of the Packers, they see a team that's together, holding hands,' " safety LeRoy Butler said. "And the word is domination."

On Sunday, the word for the Bears was "ouch!"

The Packers' 37-6 rout, their fifth straight victory over Chicago, left no doubt that Green Bay is in control of this series. Oh, the rivalry is OK. It's the Bears who are on life support. After the game, a Chicago TV crew stuck a mike in front of a drunken fan.

"The Bears ain't got no heart," he shouted, proving his grammar was as bad as his logic.

The Bears, 2-4, had plenty of heart. It was players they ran short of.

Chicago's injury list climbed to 16 by game's end. The Bears were so desperate at cornerback, first-round draft pick Walt Harris — who didn't start because of a toe injury — was forced to play when Kevin Miniefield (concussion) and Donnell Woolford (pulled hamstring) went down.

"They were really beat up," General Manager Ron Wolf said.

It was the Packers' only concession of the day.

Said Bears tackle Andy Heck, "It was a handful of big plays that did us in today."

Whose hand? The Jolly Green Giant's?

From Wayne Simmons' end zone interception, to Antonio Freeman's diving catches, to Don Beebe's 90-yard kick return, the Packers were more than a handful for the Bears. Chicago's best pass-and-catch of the game came on a fake punt that netted 16 yards.

"Ever since I got here, we've been told by Mike, 'Try to dominate. Try to put yourself in a position to dominate. Try to get good enough where you can dominate,' " defensive end Sean Jones said. "We've gotten good enough to do that. We've got good enough personnel, a good enough scheme."

Good enough, indeed. The numbers, like the victims, keep piling up. The Packers, 5-1, have outscored opponents, 204-72. Brett Favre is on pace to throw 53 TD passes. The Packers are on pace to score 544 points. The defense is on pace to force 67 turnovers. Each would be an NFL record.

The Packers aren't just winning. They're making a statement. The statement is this: "Hey, Dallas. Hey, San Francisco. We're kicking butt and and taking names. Come and get it."

The NFL has proved to be a worthy matchmaker.

The Cowboys have a date with the Packers in November. But first, there are the 49ers, who are due in Green Bay a week from today.

Said Wolf, "It's the game of the year so far."

Reggie White | DEFENSIVE LEADER

In The Trenches

BY PETE DOUGHERTY
Press-Gazette

GREEN BAY — Back on April 5, 1993, Jimmy Sexton finished negotiating the most lucrative contract of his career as an NFL players' agent, a block-buster $17 million deal for defensive end Reggie White.

Still, as he sat in his New Orleans hotel room, he felt uneasy.

He was there for the NCAA basketball Final Four, but instead of attending the North Carolina-Michigan championship game at the Superdome as he had planned, he had been negotiating on the telephone with Mike Reinfeldt, the chief financial officer of the Green Bay Packers.

After about six hours, they completed the four-year deal that made White a member of the Packers.

"I thought there was some risk involved," Sexton said. "They hadn't been to the playoffs."

In the days thereafter, Sexton was shocked by the reaction from executives around the league. He talked regularly with a number of general managers while negotiating contracts for other clients, and inevitably, White's deal with Green Bay would come up.

He said their response was almost universal.

"They were stunned and thought he sold out for the highest bid, and all those things that go along with the territory," Sexton said. "They'd tell me, 'Reggie's always talking about going to the Super Bowl. How is he going to do it in Green Bay?' "

Now that White and the Packers are going to his first Super Bowl in the fourth and final year of that contract, he feels vindicated.

"You'd have to say he was on target," Sexton said.

White was open to the criticism, not only because he went to the highest bidder, but because that team also happened to have a poor track record in the NFL standings for more than two decades.

The Packers had shown improvement at 9-7 in 1992 under first-year Coach Mike Holmgren.

But they had not played in the postseason since the strike year of 1982.

The San Francisco 49ers, on the other hand, appeared to be the frontrunner for White all along because they were the NFL's most dominating team of the 80's and 90's and had deep pockets. They made the second-best bid with a five-year, $19 million offer that, while lucrative, averaged less than the Packers' by nearly a half-million dollars ($3.8 million to $4.25 million).

Worst of all, the 49ers' offer was backloaded, meaning most of the money was to be paid in the final years of the deal.

Washington, the other finalist, was coming off a horrible 4-12 season but had won the Super Bowl just

Reggie White has spiritual reasons for wanting to stay in Green Bay after he retires.

Reggie White puts the crunch on Tampa Bay quarterback Trent Dilfer during the Packers' victory on Oct. 27.

a year before. The Redskins offered a four-year, $14 million deal.

The Packers blew away both with an astonishing contract that paid White $9 million in the first season alone — a $4.5 million signing bonus, and another $4.5 million in base salary for '93.

Even though the Packers have knocked the 49ers from the playoffs the last two years, White said his vindication runs deeper than the Super Bowl, because he also has found a new home.

Late this season he signed a contract extension that means he will finish his career with the Packers, probably in the next two or three years, even though the deal is for five more. This week he also reaffirmed that he plans to live in Wisconsin when his career ends instead of returning to his native Tennessee.

"I see the things that have happened here since I've been here," White said. "I see the acceptance of not only myself, and more importantly the word of God, I also see people respect me and my wife. In the past people only respected and were interested in me, they weren't interested in my family at all. The people up here love my wife as much as they love me. Any time I see them they say, 'We love your wife's (TV) commercial.' I say, 'No, that's my commercial.' "

White first went public with his intention to live in Wisconsin during the the playoffs for the 1995 season, after his church in Knoxville, Tenn., burned down in a suspected arson. He was overwhelmed by the goodwill and donations — which he estimates at $300,000 and growing — from people in northeastern Wisconsin.

In fact, though, he made the decision about three months before that.

Early in the 1995 season, Wisconsin endeared itself to White during an autograph session in Sheboygan.

He was stunned at the long line of people waiting there to see him, and even more taken aback when he left and they lined the highway to wave goodbye.

"I felt like the president or something," he said.

Shortly thereafter, on the Packers' bye weekend of Oct. 1, he had an appointment to preach at Believer's Church in Marshfield. People began arriving at 7 a.m. for a service that didn't start until 9.

"I began to realize, when you see God working, that's where you need to be," he said. "And I see God working up here."

White, in turn, had won the hearts of Wisconsin football fans because of his charisma and calls for racial harmony, backed up by his remarkable exploits on the football field.

Among his most memorable games was against Denver in his first year with the Packers, when at age 32 he showed he still could dominate a football game. The Packers led, 30-27, late in the fourth quarter when John Elway led a Broncos' drive to the Green Bay 43.

On back-to-back plays, third and fourth downs, White sacked Elway to preserve the win.

More startling than any of his play, which has made him the NFL's all-time sacks leader with 165 and counting, was his remarkable recovery from a torn hamstring injury in 1995. It threatened to end his season just as the Packers were heading toward the home stretch and appeared to be a crushing blow to their chances to advance deep into the playoffs and perhaps even got to the Super Bowl.

The injury occurred in the Dec. 3 game against Cincinnati, when White badly tore his left hamstring while rushing quarterback Jeff Blake. A little more than a week later, after he missed a non-strike regular-season game for the first time in his career, he tested the hamstring, both on resistance machines and with football moves.

It still was too sore to function, so he and the Packers decided he would have season-ending surgery to repair the tear.

He told his teammates about it in a teary meeting the Wednesday morning before their Dec. 16 game at New Orleans.

That night, Coach Mike Holmgren was shutting off the lights on his Christmas tree just before midnight when he saw White coming up the steps. Holmgren opened the door before White had a chance to ring the bell and joked that he thought it was Santa Claus.

"I'm getting ready to tell you something that will make you think I'm Santa Claus," White replied.

The news was, his hamstring was feeling remarkably better and he might not need the surgery after all.

Earlier that evening, barely more than 24 hours after his failed workout, he had been wrestling and running around his house with his children — his son, Jeremy, was 9 at the time, and daughter, Jecolia, was 7. Amidst the roughhousing, he noticed his hamstring suddenly felt pretty good.

He tried to test it by running in a hallway, but it wasn't long enough.

There was too much snow and ice outside, so he called the Packers' strength and conditioning coach, Kent Johnston, at about 10 p.m. to see if he could get the keys for The Don Hutson Center, which is the Packers' indoors practice field.

Johnston met him there and put him through the same football-simulation drills White could not perform the day before.

This time he could, so when they finished, he made his midnight run to Holmgren's house.

"I was still groggy," Holmgren said.

White played on a part-time basis that week against New Orleans, and slowly got better throughout the season. He already had been a fan favorite at Lambeau Field, but his amazing recovery made him a truly legendary figure in Packers' fans hearts.

Nothing could keep Reggie White down in the NFC championship game against Carolina.

Reggie White | Defensive Leader

Whether he's playing or preaching, the Packers' Reggie White gets the presidential treatment in Green Bay.

Besides playing football for the Packers, White continues to extend his ministry and other social projects, even though Green Bay doesn't have an inner city where he thinks his work can do the most good.

He's in the midst of opening a lending company for low-income people trying to start small businesses in inner-city Milwaukee, similar to a program he already has in Tennessee.

"Down South I had to use my own money to start these things," he said. "Up here people are offering money to start some of the programs we've been involved with."

His projects also are branching out to help the more fortunate.

Among other things, he's disturbed by the disproportionate number of African American athletes who get into trouble with the law. He and San Diego Padres outfielder Tony Gwynn plan to start up a player-representative agency where he and Gwynn would be unpaid advisers to young players.

White's main job, though, remains playing football for a team he never expected to join.

Holmgren and General Manager Ron Wolf had to call him several times to convince him to even visit Green Bay when he was touring prospective cities in the spring of '93. He finally relented, figuring it wasn't a long trip from his previous stop, Detroit.

The Packers, though, began to win him over at that time before they even talked about money, Sexton said.

Wolf, Holmgren and their assistant coaches didn't put on any false airs and told him that Green Bay was simply a football organization with great facilities in a small midwestern city that loved its team.

When the trip was over, White warned Sexton, "Don't be surprised if I come here."

Holmgren helped cement his relationship with White by playing off White's statements that God would tell him where he should play. While White was making up his mind, Holmgren called White and left this message on White's answering machine: "Reggie, this is God. Come to Green Bay."

Then he hung up.

Just a couple years before, Green Bay had been a place where White's coaches in Philadelphia would jokingly say they would send players if they didn't perform. Now it's his new home.

"I never imagined me being a Green Bay Packer," White said. "But I tell you what, it's been one of the most amazing experiences I've ever had in my life."

Reggie White | Defensive Leader

Reggie White knows things are going Green Bay's way during the Packers' convincing win over the Broncos on Dec. 8.

Packers	6	0	8	6	3	23
49ers	0	17	0	3	0	20

Jacke Nails Niners

BY PETE DOUGHERTY
Press-Gazette

GREEN BAY, OCT. 14, 1996 — With the game on the line, Packers coach Mike Holmgren trusted his instinct.

It proved to be a trustworthy source.

In their biggest game this season, the Packers defeated San Francisco Monday night, 23-20, in overtime because Holmgren made a gutsy call that worked.

There were still more than 11 minutes left in OT when he had to decide whether Chris Jacke should try a 53-yard field goal. There was good reason not to attempt the kick.

If Jacke missed, after all, the 49ers would get a short field, starting at the spot of the kick, their own 43. That's only a couple of completions from a possible game-winning kick of their own.

With Craig Hentrich holding, Chris Jacke boots the game-winning field goal (left) and follows its path.

It was fourth-and-5 and Holmgren consulted his instinct, honed by 26 years of coaching football in high school, college and the NFL. It told him to go for the kill.

"I figured, shoot, let's try it," Holmgren said.

They did, and the Packers won.

That instinct to go for the jugular was in contrast to what 49ers coach George Seifert decided to do near the end of regulation.

Seifert played it safe in the last two minutes of regulation when he had quarterback Elvis Grbac down the ball in the middle of the field on third down, setting up a straight-on field goal rather than taking one shot at the end zone from the 10-yard line. It was the safe play and gave the 49ers a 20-17 lead, but it also left Packers quarterback Brett Favre with 1 minute 50 seconds and needing only to get into field-goal position for the tie.

Holmgren, on the other hand, took the riskier route and went for the big score when he got the chance. Favre took the Packers to San Francisco's 13 with only 30 seconds remaining, and he tried three straight passes into the end zone before Jacke tied the game with a 31-yard field goal.

"I mean, you get inside the 20 down there, get that close and settle for a field goal?" receiver Don Beebe said. "No, we were trying to win the game."

Then, when it came time to make the field-goal decision in overtime, Holmgren didn't hesitate. No time out, no deliberation. He sent Jacke and the field-goal unit onto the field almost immediately after Favre had thrown the ball away to avoid a sack on third down.

Perhaps the decision was made easier after watching his defense in perhaps its finest hour. It had limited the 49ers to only 75 yards and three points in the second half, with the field goal set up by an interception at the Packers' 12.

"Mike made (the decision), and it was the right one," said Fritz Shurmur, the Packers' defensive coor-

Game 7 | PACKERS 23, 49ERS 20

Team leaders Brett Favre (left) and Reggie White embrace following Chris Jacke's game-winning field goal in overtime.

dinator. "Nolan (Cromwell, the special-teams coach) was comfortable with the distance, and Mike was comfortable with the distance. If (the defense) had to go back out there, we'd have to fight and find a way to knock 'em outta there."

The kick could end up doing wonders for Jacke. In the last two years, his accuracy has slipped a bit from the high standards he had set up earlier in his career. In 1994 and '95 combined, he made 73.5 percent of his field goals (36-for-49) after making 78.4 percent his first five years.

This season, he was 7-for-10 going into Monday night, including missing a 38-yarder in the kicker-

friendly conditions of the Kingdome in Seattle. And he missed an extra point last week at Chicago.

Among other things, he was stung in the Seattle game when Holmgren passed up a 52-yard field goal in the second quarter, before Jacke had even missed a kick that day.

"A lot of people — the press and some fans — have been giving him a hard time since his misses at Tampa Bay and Seattle," said Craig Hentrich, the Packers' punter and Jacke's holder. "Maybe this will get them off his back."

Jacke went into the kick having made more than 50 percent (16-for-25) of his attempts from 50 yards

Beebe Speeds Into Spotlight

BY CHRIS HAVEL
Press-Gazette

Don Beebe has had big games before, but he has never enjoyed one as much as the Packers' 23-20 victory against San Francisco on Monday night.

The Packers' fastest player became an overnight sensation by catching 11 passes for 220 yards and a touchdown. He had two catches for 20 yards to set up Chris Jacke's 31-yard field goal to tie the game at 20 in the fourth quarter. Then, Beebe hauled in a 13-yard reception to help set up Jacke's 53-yard game winner with 11:19 to play in overtime.

The victory moves the Packers, 6-1, into sole possession of first place in the NFC Central. It also moves Beebe into the Packers' record books. His 220 yards is third-best in team history behind Billy Howton, who had 257 yards vs. the Rams in 1956, and Don Hutson, who had 237 vs. Brooklyn in 1943.

"I had four touchdowns in a game when I was with Buffalo, but we blew Pittsburgh out," he said. "So the way we won this game made it much more enjoyable to help out the team."

Beebe, 31, came into the game when Robert Brooks suffered a season-ending knee injury on the Packers' first play from scrimmage. He went on to post the team's first 200-yard receiving game since James Lofton had 206 in a blizzard at Denver on Oct. 15, 1984.

"The little guy can play, can't he," Packers coach Mike Holmgren said. "What a great effort. We needed it."

Beebe's biggest play, perhaps, came midway through

The Packers' Don Beebe hauls in a 54-yard pass from Brett Favre that set up a first-quarter field goal.

the third quarter when he made a diving catch at the 49ers' 30-yard line, got up and ran untouched into the end zone for a 59-yard touchdown.

Nobody was going to catch Beebe, who ran the 40-yard dash in 4.25 seconds this past offseason.

"He can scoot," Packers tight end Mark Chmura said. "He's almost as fast as I am."

of more, though he hadn't tried one from that distance this season. At 53 yards, it would tie for the second-longest field goal in Packers' history, behind the 54-yarder he made at Detroit's Silverdome on Jan. 2, 1994.

His teammates on the field-goal unit didn't say much to him, and it helped that there was no timeout other than the stop in play. Hentrich assured him the hold would be good, and he saw a confident look when Jacke said, "Here's the spot. Let's kick it through."

"I knew it (was good) as soon as he hit it," Hentrich said. "I don't need to look up. I can tell by the sound now."

Said Jacke: "It was probably one of the better balls I've kicked in a long time."

It came on a day when Jacke kicked five field goals

and became the Packers' second-leading all-time scorer with 763 points. That surpasses Paul Hornung (760 points), with Don Hutson (823) in the lead.

The last two kicks — the 31-yarder to tie with eight seconds left and the game winner — were about as pressure-filled as field goals can get during the regular season.

This, after all, was against the NFL's premier team of the 80's and 90's, the 49ers. And it was in the national spotlight of Monday Night Football in a game that matched probably the two best teams in the league, at least the best through the first seven weeks of the season.

"He'll sleep well," Hentrich said. "That's the ultimate. And if you miss it, you want to walk to the other sideline. That's the life of a kicker."

Jerry Rice caught two touchdown passes, but on this play he was humbled by Packers linebacker Wayne Simmons.

Game 7 | OCTOBER 14, 1996

Injured Trio Didn't Miss Celebration

BY CHRIS HAVEL
Press-Gazette

The instant Chris Jacke's 53-yard field goal attempt split the uprights, the place went wild. There were hugs and high-fives. Tears and cheers. Shouts and screams and all sorts of craziness from men in green and gold jerseys.

Such was the scene inside the Packers' training room.

The joy felt by a trio of injured players mirrored that of a record 60,716 fans at Lambeau Field after the Packers' 23-20 overtime win against the 49ers.

Robert Brooks, Edgar Bennett and Earl Dotson weren't on the field, or in the stands, for that matter, but they were into Monday night's game.

Just as the fans stayed with their team despite a 17-6 halftime deficit, so did these players, despite being knocked out of action. Yeah, they were in serious pain. But they didn't need a paramedic. They were getting the best medicine in the world. They were getting a Packers victory.

"When (Jacke) made the kick, those guys raised the roof," said Jason Helgeson, a 24-year-old training room intern who was tending to the wounded. "It was pretty electric."

Helgeson, a UW-Green Bay graduate in his second year with the team, said the training room atmosphere was never down.

"They weren't worried about their shoulders or their knees or anything," he said. "Brooks was in a lot of pain. They all were. But they weren't thinking about themselves."

Say this for the Packers: They stick together in

Injured Robert Brooks exits Lambeau Field sidelines.

rehab and in health. It's the kind of reaction you'd expect, especially from three guys who epitomize team play. They didn't get to be interviewed by Leslie Visser or draw breathless praise from Frank, Dan and Al.

They didn't care. Their only regret, it seems, was that this 3½-hour drama didn't play out long enough for them to heal and return, though with every passing commercial that seemed possible.

They didn't have time for sympathy or self-pity. They were too busy watching, praying, and finally celebrating the team's biggest win in a special season.

This was as good as convalescence gets.

"A 53-yard field goal?" said Bennett, his left shoulder in a sling. "I was high-fivin' with my good arm!"

THE ROAD TO SUPER BOWL XXXI | **55**

Packers	3	10	0	0	13
Bucanneers	0	0	0	7	7

Paying A Painful Price

By Pete Dougherty
Press-Gazette

GREEN BAY, OCT. 27, 1996 — The price of victory has grown steep for the Green Bay Packers.

In each of their last two games, they've won the battle, knocking off San Francisco in an overtime thriller two weeks ago and beating Tampa Bay in a pedestrian 13-7 game Sunday.

But while the victories have pushed the Packers to 7-1, they've also taken a huge bite out of their offense, which came into Sunday as the highest scoring in the NFL.

In a season where so much had fallen into place for them, the Packers suddenly face playing most of the second half of the year without their two best receivers. Against the 49ers they suffered the painful loss of flanker Robert Brooks to a season-ending knee injury. Against the Buccaneers, they lost the man who replaced him as their go-to receiver, Antonio Freeman, to a broken left forearm that will sideline him from four to six weeks.

"Early in the year I though this team had more talent and depth than any team I've played on," said Keith Jackson, who had been to the playoffs with Philadelphia and Miami. "But that's been blown away pretty fast."

Only nine weeks ago, the Packers' deepest position was receiver. They were loaded enough that Anthony Morgan, a part-time starter last year, became expendable, even though they kept an extra, sixth receiver on their final roster.

"In training camp everybody was talking about who we're going to get rid of," said rookie Derrick Mayes. "Now we're talking about who we're going to get back. It's crazy."

The most important returnee will be Terry Mickens, who has been out all regular season with a badly sprained ankle that has been slow to heal. He has practiced the past two weeks, and the Packers are hoping he will be ready next week when Detroit visits Lambeau Field. The third-year pro had been in the running for the starting spot opposite Brooks until his injury late in training camp.

Even with today's re-signing of Morgan, much of the responsibility of replacing Brooks and Freeman will fall to the players who filled in against Tampa Bay.

For the final three quarters, the Packers' starting receiver tandem was Desmond Howard at flanker and Don Beebe at split end. Howard caught five passes for 30 yards, and Holmgren said he probably will remain

Edgar Bennett carried the offensive load, rushing for 93 yards on 20 attempts — a 4.7 average per carry.

at flanker. Beebe had a quiet day with three receptions after catching 11 passes against the 49ers.

Mayes, a rookie, also will get a close look because of his intriguing talent. The second-round draft pick played well enough in training camp that the Packers thought he would be a contributor before the year was out. Now he will be by necessity, though his development was set back in training camp by a separated left shoulder two weeks before the regular-season opener.

He's been back playing for the last three games, and after catching his first NFL pass against the 49ers, he caught two more passes Sunday for 20 yards as the No. 3 receiver.

"They say sometimes you get what you ask for but not when you request it," Mayes said. "I've asked for an opportunity to show my stuff, and now I've got it."

The Packers went into Sunday's game as the NFL's highest-scoring team, but 13 points was their season low.

Even before Freeman was hurt, their plan had been to run against the Buccaneers, and they did that well enough most of the day that Favre's first game this season without a touchdown pass didn't cost them. Halfback Edgar Bennett had 20 carries for 93 yards, and he combined with Dorsey Levens and William Henderson to average 4.2 yards a carry.

But in coming weeks, against highly regarded defenses such as Dallas and Kansas City, the Packers surely will have to lean heavily on their passing game.

On Sunday, they gave a glimpse of what might be expected. For instance, Jackson and Mark Chmura played in two-tight end formations more than they had in recent weeks, and Chmura ended a two-game reception drought by catching three passes for 59 yards.

The players and coaching staff have great confi-

Antonio Freeman waits for assistance after suffering a broken left forearm on a hit by Bucs safety Melvin Johnson.

Packers Have Chance To Prove Their Depth

BY CHRIS HAVEL
Press-Gazette

Another game. Another victory. Another injury. Say this for the Packers: They take a hit and keep on clicking.

First Robert Brooks, now Antonio Freeman. Green Bay's receiving corps — or is that corpse? — used to make us marvel at the wonders of the human hand. Now, it is conducting a weekly anatomy class, teaching us more than we wanted to know about patellar tendons and ulna bones.

After Sunday's game Freeman said he was "heartbroken." And what's the recovery time for that?

The Packers' three-receiver package isn't Brooks, Freeman and Mickens. It's Snap, Crackle and Pop.

Such is life in the NFL, where the weekly injury report typically runs longer than a Clinton-Dole debate, and is more informative.

It is why quality depth is essential to success.

And why Packers fans needn't panic just yet.

Their team is one of the NFL's deepest. Now they have a chance to prove it.

"Buddy Ryan used to have a saying: 'The best thing some guys have going for them is they don't have to play,' " defensive end Sean Jones said. "We don't have any guys like that on this team."

Desmond Howard, come on down. You are the next contestant on Flanker For A Day, the game where weakside blocks and slant routes can make punt returning seem like child's play.

dence in Holmgren's West Coast offense, which relies more than anything on the quarterback's ability to check from one receiver to the next until he finds someone open. The problem is, their greatest strength had been the array of weapons Favre had available. Now two of his best weapons are gone.

"Maybe we have to re-evaluate how we do some things," Holmgren said. "The things is, you have the MVP in the league playing quarterback, so you don't want to take the ball out of his hands too much."

The Packers feel fortunate they at least will get Freeman back late in the season. If he's back in six weeks, he'll have the final three games of the regular season to shake the rust before the playoffs begin.

The injury happened late in the first quarter, as Freeman tried to catch a pass at the goal line while running through the middle of the Bucs' secondary. Freeman said Favre saw safety Melvin Johnson closing in on the pass pattern, so he threw a low pass that only Freeman could catch.

Johnson hit Freeman helmet to helmet, but what caused the injury was that Johnson's knee landed squarely against Freeman's left forearm. Freeman said he didn't feel any pain, and after watching a replay of the hit he said it was a clean play.

"I felt my arm go numb, and it sent me into shock," he said.

It was Freeman's first start at flanker. The second-year pro went into Sunday's game as the Packers' leading receiver with 31 receptions.

At halftime, he telephoned Brooks at home for solace, then watched the second half from the sidelines with his arm in a sling. He was scheduled to have surgery today to have a metal plate implanted to speed the break's healing.

"I was heartbroken," he said of the injury. "This was an opportunity for me to establish myself as the go-to guy in this offense for Brett Favre."

Packers	7	7	14	0	28
Lions	3	7	0	8	18

Subs Catch On Quickly

BY PETE DOUGHERTY
Press-Gazette

GREEN BAY, NOV. 3, 1996 — Three weeks ago Don Beebe was a kickoff returner and part-time player, and Terry Mickens was an injured and forgotten man.

Now, they're the productive starting receivers for a Super Bowl contender that at 8-1 will finish this week no worse than tied for the best record in the NFL.

In the first of what probably will be at least four games as the starting receiving tandem, Beebe and Mickens combined for 11 receptions, 158 yards and three touchdowns in the Green Bay Packers' 28-18 win over Detroit on Sunday.

The Packers went into this game wondering how much their offense would suffer from the injury losses of their two best receivers, Robert Brooks and Antonio Freeman. They came out with four touchdown passes, 355 yards in total offense, and confirmation that their receiving corps indeed is uncommonly deep.

Though Favre was as sharp as ever (24-for-35 passing for 281 yards and four touchdowns), circumstances helped make Mickens and Beebe the stars of the day.

Three weeks ago, the Packers lost Brooks — who caught 102 passes last season — to a devastating season-ending knee injury. Last week, Freeman was knocked out of the lineup for at least four games with a broken left forearm.

With his 11-reception game against San Francisco, Beebe proved worthy of a starting assignment. Coach Mike Holmgren moved him to the featured flanker position, even though he had worked mostly at split end since joining the Packers in the offseason.

The other starting spot was left open for Mickens, Anthony Morgan and Derrick Mayes. Each had distinct strengths and weaknesses.

Mickens has been in the offense for three years, but his health was shaky because he was coming off a severe ankle injury that had sidelined him the first eight games.

Morgan was a part-time starter last year but had not played football since the Packers cut him at the end of training camp. They re-signed him last week.

And Mayes, though gifted, is a rookie who lost valuable practice time earlier in the season because of a separated shoulder.

Mickens was the preferred choice, because he was experienced and, despite his injury, in good shape. The question was his left ankle.

The Packers had estimated he would miss six games when he hurt it in camp. He ended up missing eight, and though they were trying to bring him back slowly, Freeman's injury made it imperative Mickens play this week.

On Saturday evening, the coaching staff informed him he was the starter. Morgan would be the No. 3 receiver, and Mayes would play in four-receiver sets.

Not only was Sunday Mickens' first game of the season, but it also was the first start of a three-year

Terry Mickens celebrates one of his two touchdown catches in his first NFL start.

Packers tight end Keith Jackson rumbles past Lions safety Bennie Blades on one of his three catches on the day.

career in which he had caught a total of seven passes and played mainly on special teams.

"It didn't matter whether I was starting or not," Mickens said. "I'd prepare the same way."

After the game, Mickens said the ankle is getting close but is not yet at full strength. There were some patterns he couldn't cut sharply enough Sunday.

Nevertheless, he set the tone on the Packers' first

completion of the day. He converted a third-and-5 when he caught a short drag route over the middle and fought through the tackle of cornerback Greg Jeffries for the first down. It immediately endeared him to his teammates and the Lambeau Field crowd.

"People want to see blue-collar guys who go out there and fight for every inch and every yard," Beebe said.

Mickens finished with seven receptions for 52 yards

Barry Sanders ran for 105 yards in the first half, but the Packers put the clamps on the Lions' star in the second half.

and touchdown receptions of 1 and 6 yards. It presumably will be enough to keep him the starter for next week's game at Kansas City.

"That's every player's dream, to get in and play, and not only play, but play well," he said.

Beebe had fewer catches (four), but he had the back-breaker, a 65-yard touchdown on a play the Packers' coaching staff had put in just for this game. It gave Green Bay a 28-10 lead late in the third quarter and showed some quick-strike capability even without Brooks and Freeman.

When Beebe signed with the Packers last April, he set himself up for a tough fight just to make the team.

Within a month, the Packers drafted Mayes in the second round. They also had Morgan coming back from a season in which he started eight games and knew Freeman was ready to make a run at a starting job.

Beebe won the fight for a roster spot in large part because he returned kickoffs and Morgan didn't. Now he and Mickens are the latest standouts after getting plugged into Holmgren's West Coast offense. He's the team's second-leading receiver (25 receptions).

"This is definitely a receiver's offense," Beebe said.

Until Beebe's 65-yard touchdown, the Packers looked more like they had the past few seasons, when they relied heavily on screens to their running backs and short passes to their receivers.

Eight players caught passes, and the next longest after Beebe's was for 17 yards. Tight ends Mark Chmura and Keith Jackson combined for six catches, and running back Edgar Bennett, William Henderson and Dorsey Levens combined for seven.

"We went in with the idea of spreading the ball around a little bit more because of our wide receiver situation," Holmgren said.

Game 9 | Packers 28, Lions 18

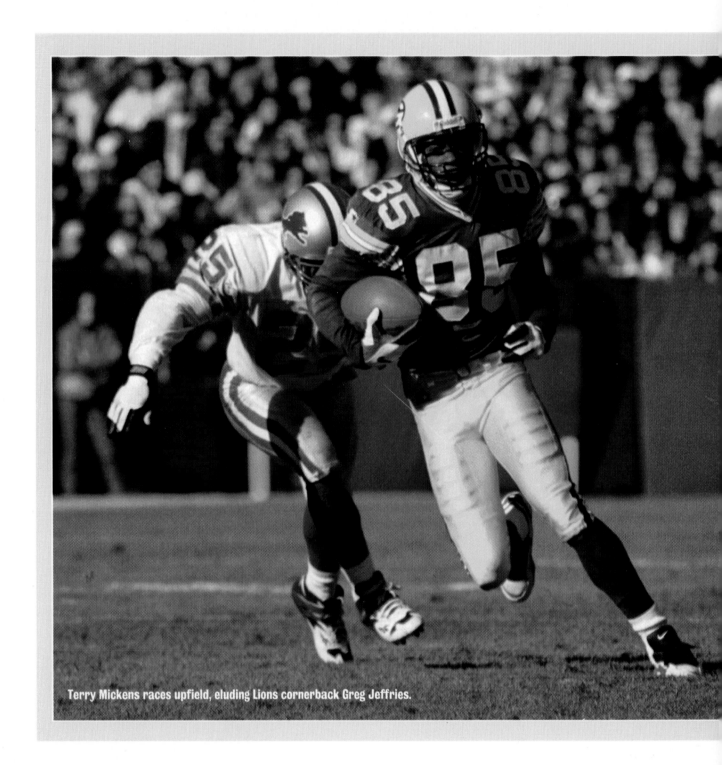

Terry Mickens races upfield, eluding Lions cornerback Greg Jeffries.

Favre Makes New Targets Feel At Home

BY CHRIS HAVEL
Press-Gazette

You suspected the Lions were finished when Scott Mitchell showed up at a Halloween party dressed as Wayne Fontes. You knew they were finished when Brett Favre showed up at Lambeau Field dressed as himself.

The NFL's reigning MVP has reduced the task of analyzing his mistakes to so much nit-picking. An overthrow here. An underthrow there. The occasional bad decision. No, Favre isn't perfect. But he isn't Don Majkowski, either.

At age 27, Favre has displayed the singular quality that separates the good players from the great ones. He makes his teammates better.

It happened in Sunday's 28-18 victory over Detroit. He completed 24 of 35 passes for 281 yards and four touchdowns. Never mind that his primary targets were a Carolina castoff and a nondescript pro who matched his career total for catches (seven) in a single afternoon.

Make no mistake. Don Beebe and Terry Mickens are quality receivers, but they are not Robert Brooks and Antonio Freeman. If they were, they'd have been in the starting lineup on Sept. 1 at Tampa Bay.

Favre doesn't seem to care, as long as someone is on the other end of his passes. He treats his receivers' identities as minor details.

He throws. They catch. It's a pretty simple deal.

By game's end, he helped Mickens become a household name and Beebe continue his sprint into the ranks of the NFL's top deep threats at 31. Still, the general reaction to Favre's performance was a yawn. That includes Favre.

"I'm actually a little disappointed we didn't do more," he said. "We had a chance to really put up some big numbers today. But we won the game."

Hmmm. Four touchdowns, 281 yards and a 68.6 completion percentage. If those numbers don't excite you, try turning on the TV and watching the Chiefs' Steve Bono or the Vikings' Brad Johnson.

There was a time when Favre's stats against the Lions would've drawn a standing ovation, a tickertape parade, or perhaps even something really valuable like stock in cheeseheads and Title Towels.

Now, such a performance is considered routine, ho-hum, so-so. This is another quality associated with the great ones. They make it look easy.

If Favre was concerned about the state of his receiving corps — and he had good reason to be — he didn't let anybody know it. Publicly, he said and did everything he could to boost the confidence of Mickens, Derrick Mayes & Co. Privately, he took time from his own preparation to assist them in theirs.

He accepted Holmgren's criticism that he occasionally tried to do too much Sunday with a nod, saying, "That's fair enough." He accepted the additional responsibility that comes with losing talented receivers such as Brooks and Freeman in similar fashion.

No hissing and moaning here. Only the question, "What can I do to make us better?"

Lately, all that is required of Favre is stepping onto the field.

As terrific as the Lions' Barry Sanders was on Sunday, Favre was the better player, a considerable accomplishment on a day when nobody confused the Packers' offensive line with The Seven Blocks of Granite.

Brett Favre, who was sacked four times, contemplates the loss to the Chiefs on the Arrowhead Stadium sidelines.

Chiefs	3	17	7	0	27
Packers	3	3	7	7	20

Chiefs Crush Packers

By Pete Dougherty
Press-Gazette

KANSAS CITY, NOV. 10, 1996 — For the first time in a long time, the Green Bay Packers ran into a defense that had too many weapons.

The Kansas City Chiefs on Sunday featured Neil Smith and Derrick Thomas rushing Packers quarterback Brett Favre from the outside. They had cornerbacks Dale Carter and James Hasty playing rough, belly-to-belly defense on Green Bay's wide receivers. They had the element of surprise with an array of blitzes the Chiefs hadn't shown this year, and they had the deafening Arrowhead Stadium crowd to keep the Packers' offensive linemen from getting a jump on the snap count.

It added up to a 27-20 loss for the Packers that, despite the seven-point margin, was as sound a defeat as they have suffered since the Dallas Cowboys beat them by 10 points in October 1995.

"This is a tough place to play," said Packers receiver Don Beebe. "(The loss) is something a championship-caliber team will put behind them and go on to the next week."

The defeat drops the Packers to 8-2, but losses by San Francisco, Philadelphia and Washington leave Green Bay with the best record in the NFC.

The costliest part of it, though, is it further depleted the Packers' arsenal. They already are without starting receivers Robert Brooks and Antonio Freeman because of recent injuries, and on Sunday they lost tight end Mark Chmura for the final three quarters and surely longer because of a sprained arch he suf-

fered halfway through the first quarter.

Although Coach Mike Holmgren said the injury will not require surgery, a strained arch can be serious. Holmgren said he didn't know how long Chmura will be sidelined, but all signs point to him not being ready to play soon. Chmura was unable to put any weight on his foot coming off the field and was on crutches after the game.

"Chewy's a big part of this offense," said his partner at tight end, Keith Jackson. "We're comfortable in the two-tight ends (alignment), and his blocking at the point of attack, he definitely played a role in that."

The Packers said they did not change their play calling with Chmura out, though third-stringer Jeff Thomason only took a handful of snaps in the second half in the two-tight end offense.

Nevertheless, it deprives them of one of Favre's favorite targets at a time when they appeared ready to lean on him, with Brooks out for the year and Freeman expected to miss two more games.

"I'm not worried about our weapons," General Manager Ron Wolf said. "We'll have weapons as long as No. 4 can stand up."

The Chiefs made it their No. 1 priority on Sunday to limit No. 4 (Favre), and they are as well equipped for that as any team in the league, with Smith and

Thomas as their defensive ends on passing downs. The Chiefs sacked Favre four times, induced an intentional grounding penalty on him on another play and had him under pressure regularly.

They surprised the Packers with a blitzing scheme they had not shown this season. They blitzed from several different positions — Hasty, a cornerback, had one of their sacks — and kept the Packers in check for nearly the entire first half. After a 50-yard drive that yielded a field goal on its first drive, Green Bay had only 79 yards the rest of the first half.

"Half the time, I didn't see what was coming," said Aaron Taylor, the Packers' left guard. "There were a lot of people running around."

But many teams have blitzed the Packers this season, and usually Favre has made them pay. The Chiefs, though, offer an unusual problem because they have Smith and Thomas leading the rush.

Smith didn't have a big day against right tackle Earl Dotson, but he made a huge play on the first snap of the second half when he sacked Favre from behind and caused a fumble Thomas recovered. That led to the touchdown that gave the Chiefs a 27-6 lead.

The Packers tried to help contain Thomas by keeping a running back in as an extra blocker on several plays, yet Thomas managed two sacks and a number of pressures. Thomas is a linebacker who lines up as a down lineman on passing downs, and when the Chiefs' lead grew to 27-6 in the third quarter, left tackles John Michels and Ken Ruettgers saw more and more of him the rest of the way.

"We've been banged up at the tackles," Favre said. "That doesn't help when there are two of the best pass rushers in the league coming from the outside. Plus, we can't hear (because of the crowd noise).

Carter and Hasty played as tough and physical a game as the Packers' cornerbacks did last season in their playoff win at San Francisco. It's no coincidence that the

When Favre Goes Down, So Do Packers

By Eric Goska
Press-Gazette

The wide receivers in the Packers' offense might be replaceable, but when the quarterback goes down, the unit struggles.

The Chiefs sacked Brett Favre four times Sunday and hurried him on numerous other occasions. Favre threw one interception, lost 21 yards on an intentional grounding call and had a string of six straight incompletions during the span in which Kansas City scored 17 unanswered points.

Favre also lost a fumble to open the second half that Greg Hill turned into six points on the Chiefs' following play from scrimmage.

Over the years, the Packers' offense has rolled on despite changes to the receiving corps. Sterling Sharpe went down and Robert Brooks stepped in. Jackie Harris departed for Tampa Bay and Mark Chmura made the Pro Bowl.

This year, Green Bay has overcome the loss of Brooks and Antonio Freeman.

The key to the Packers' offense is Favre. When he spends more time on his back than reading defenses, the attack is halted. Favre has been sacked four or more times on 14 occasions since arriving in Green Bay. His record is 4-10 in those games.

Kansas City got to Favre once on four different drives. All four drives ended without scores. Craig Hentrich punted three times and Favre's fumble was the other.

Brett Favre dances around the pursuit of Chiefs linebacker Anthony Davis. Favre still managed 310 yards passing.

Packers' three leading receivers were running backs Dorsey Levens, William Henderson and Edgar Bennett, who combined for 14 of the Packers' 27 receptions.

"They took away our outside game," said Sherman Lewis, the Packers' offensive coordinator.

Carter is one of the NFL's best cornerbacks and was on Beebe much of the day. He helped limit Beebe to three receptions and broke up two passes, including recovering on a fourth-quarter bomb after Beebe had slipped past him and Favre had thrown on target.

"(Carter) has all the tools," Beebe said. "He has very long arms. He's got good size (6-foot-1, 188

pounds), he's a physical guy, and he can jump, as you saw on that long pass. And he has great speed. I mean, that's a good player."

Beebe did have one big play, when Favre audibled on a blitz and hit him over Hasty for a 25-yard touchdown in the third quarter. But most of the day, Carter and Hasty successfully battled Beebe, Terry Mickens and Anthony Morgan at the line of scrimmage and slowed their path downfield better that any other team has this year.

"You have to give them a lot of credit," Morgan said. "They get in your face and challenge you. And after the 5-yard chuck (zone), they get some extra hits in."

Brett Favre can't brush off Cowboys linebacker Broderick Thomas while being sacked during the second quarter.

Cowboys	6	9	0	6	21
Packers	0	0	0	6	6

Cowboys Sack Pack

By Pete Dougherty
Press-Gazette

Irving, Nov. 18, 1996 — As Green Bay Packers General Manager Ron Wolf made his way down to the field near the end of yet another loss at Texas Stadium, he could hear the Dallas Cowboys' radio announcers blasting through the concourse.

The Cowboys were nearly finished heaping another shovel full of frustrations on Wolf and the Packers with a 21-6 win, their seventh straight victory over Green Bay in the past 3¾ years.

It left the Packers facing really only one issue that mattered afterward: What will it take for them to beat this team? And the only answer, after a seventh trip to Dallas that had a different story line but the same result, was the hope that things would be different if the teams met at Lambeau Field.

"(The announcers) said they would kick our (butts) in Lambeau," Wolf said. "We'd just like to have that opportunity."

The defeat left the Packers in unfamiliar territory in 1996: Their first back-to-back losses of the season and facing questions about whether their injury-depleted offense can hold up when tested by the best defense the league has to offer.

The Packers came into the weekend the NFL's top-scoring team, but in losses to Dallas and Kansas City the past two games they have averaged only 13 points. They will get some relief next week, when they play at St. Louis, which came into this past weekend with the 29th-rated defense in yards allowed and 28th in points allowed.

They also will get some of their key players back in the next few weeks, though they have to play the rest of this season without flanker Robert Brooks, who is out with a knee injury. They expect to get receiver Antonio Freeman back from a broken forearm after one more game, and tight end Mark Chmura back from a torn arch in two to four weeks.

Nevertheless, the Cowboys maintained their recent dominance over Green Bay even in a season in which the 8-3 Packers finally had gained the edge over the 7-4 Cowboys in the NFC standings.

The Packers' 1996 season, which had gotten off to such a spectacular start, has hit its first big bump, not only because they've lost two straight games, but because they still haven't shaken the Cowboys' albatross.

"This will be a huge test," said Don Beebe, the Packers' starting flanker. "I think we'll be fine. We're down now, sure. This is a tough loss. But this team has had a knack of putting things behind it. All we have to do is win (the final five) games and we'll play

Game 11 | Cowboys 21, Packers 6

them again (at home) in January."

In the past six wins over Green Bay, the Cowboys had won basically because they had more firepower. The Cowboys came into the weekend with the NFL's top-rated defense for yards allowed and fifth in points given up. The Packers' defense was second and first.

Without Brooks, Freeman and Chmura, the Packers came into this game preferring their matchup with tight end Keith Jackson over any of their receivers against the Cowboys' outstanding cornerback duo of Deion Sanders and Kevin Smith. Jackson had his moments and struck for seven receptions for 98 yards.

But the Packers were unable to sustain anything until they had become desperate, trailing, 18-0, with eight minutes to play in the game. They gained 123 of their 254 yards in total offense in that final eight minutes, and scored their only points on a 3-yard lob pass from Brett Favre to rookie Derrick Mayes to avert what would have been Mike Holmgren's first shutout in his five seasons as Packers coach.

"Who's the No. 1 defense now?" asked Sanders, the Cowboys' All-Pro cover man. "We've proved we're No. 1 tonight."

"It's only the third game we've lost," defensive end Sean Jones said. "There's a lot of teams, including Dallas, who wish they only had lost three times."

Packers safety LeRoy Butler is flying high in his pursuit of Cowboys quarterback Troy Aikman.

Packers Must Avoid Return Trip To Dallas

By Chris Havel

Press-Gazette

Say hello to Barry Switzer, the life of an otherwise dull party.

The Cowboys' coach woke up, took the lampshade off his head and accomplished more in 20 seconds than the Packers' offense did the entire evening. With one classless stunt, he managed to rub the Packers' noses in it and stick his kicker's foot in his mouth.

The heck with coaching. Switzer ought to rent himself out on New Year's Eve.

That said, the Packers learned a couple of lessons in Monday night's 21-6 loss, some of which might even be valuable if and when these two teams renew the NFL's most bitter, lopsided rivalry, if there can be such a thing.

First, never underestimate Switzer's ability to sink to new depths. Second, never underestimate the Cowboy's ability, period. Dallas was clearly the better team in its seventh straight victory over Green Bay during Coach Mike Holmgren's otherwise exemplary tenure.

If Switzer's decision to have Chris Boniol attempt an NFL record-tying seventh field goal in any way detracted from the game's first 59 minutes and 40 seconds, the Packers ought to be grateful. On a night when their defense was stingy in the red zone, their offense rarely got there.

"Defensively we did a good job," Packers All-Pro Reggie White said. "But we allowed them to get too many field goals."

Four too many, to be exact. While White's mad dash toward the Cowboys' sideline epitomized the Packers'

frustrations, the first-half statistics foreshadowed them.

The Cowboys outgained the Packers 213 to 61 through two quarters. The fact that the Dallas defense limited Brett Favre & Co. to 22 yards passing in their first five possessions proves Robert Brooks, Antonio Freeman and Mark Chmura aren't merely indisposed, but indispensable.

"They had nothing to hang their hats on," Switzer said of Green Bay's offense. "It was total domination by our defense."

On this point, there can be no debate.

A Dallas defense that lost Russell Maryland, Larry Brown, Charles Haley, Robert Jones, Dixon Edwards and Brock Marion still found a way to get it done with ex-Packers George Teague, Fred Strickland and an anonymous trio of Randall Godfrey, Jim Swantz and Shante Carver.

That same Dallas defense currently ranks No. 1 in the NFL.

What the Cowboys don't have, though, is control of their own destiny when it comes to capturing the NFC's home-field advantage in the playoffs. Because of receiver Michael Irvin's selfish offseason indulgences, a slow start has forced them to need some help.

The Packers, 8-3, don't plan to do the 7-4 Cowboys any favors.

As terrific a disaster as Monday night's game was for Green Bay, the Packers now seem more intent than ever on putting together a five-game winning streak.

"The object is to get into the playoffs and there is still five more games," Packers defensive end Sean Jones said. "We want to get Dallas or whoever we play, up in Lambeau."

Packers	0	3	14	7	24
Rams	0	9	0	0	9

Defense To The Rescue

By Pete Dougherty
Press-Gazette

St. Louis, Nov. 14, 1996—Lawrence Phillips took the first handoff of the second half and ran smack into 350-pound nose tackle Gilbert Brown of the Green Bay Packers.

With that one hit to open the third quarter, which knocked Phillips for a 1-yard loss, Brown changed the tone of what had been a drab day for the Packers against the St. Louis Rams on Sunday.

On the very next snap, cornerback Doug Evans read rookie quarterback Tony Banks for an interception that he turned into a 32-yard touchdown, and in two plays the Packers had awakened on their way to a 24-9 win that ended their two-game losing streak.

Early Sunday, Brown was taking fluid intravenously because he had a bad case of the flu, and the Packers weren't sure if he'd play that night. But when they came out at the start of the second half determined to stop the Rams' running game — Phillips had gained 23 yards on six carries on St. Louis' lone touchdown drive late in the first half — Brown was their stopper.

"You talk about (giving out) the game ball, it should go to that guy over there," said safety Eugene Robinson as he pointed across the Packers' locker room at Brown. "He threw the center out of the way and smacked the crap out of (Phillips). I think that was the play of the game."

If Brown's stop set the tone, Evans' interception provided a more tangible life for a Packers team that trailed, 9-3, and had endured a horrendous first half in which their struggling offense gained only 65 yards.

The Packers baited Banks into the interception by having one of their safeties, LeRoy Butler, fake a blitz, and instead sent their other safety, Robinson. To get rid of the ball quickly, Banks tried to throw quickly to receiver J.T. Thomas on a slant pattern, but Evans saw it the entire way. He stepped in front of Thomas for the interception and ran untouched for the 32-yard score, the first touchdown of his career.

Suddenly, the dismal first half was forgotten.

"I read the quarterback, read the receiver and looked for the ball," Evans said. "It wasn't that hard. Read, read, ball. It's everything we work on in practice."

Besides giving the Packers their first lead since their Nov. 3 win against Detroit, it also gave their slumping offense a boost. The Packers on their next four possessions gained 188 yards and were in scoring position each time. Twice quarterback Brett Favre connected on touchdown passes, and twice he was intercepted in the end zone.

"It's crazy how emotion can play into it," receiver Don Beebe said. "If we could learn to play with emotion like that every game and get that kind of spark —

Rams quarterback Tony Banks feels the heat as he is pressured by Packers LeRoy Butler (36) and Reggie White.

we've been waiting three of four games for that kind of spark, and Doug provided it that play. It was a turn of emotion like I've never seen."

Favre went on to find the rhythm of the Packers' ball-control passing game that had been missing the past two weeks in losses at Kansas City and Dallas. In the second half against the Rams he went 15-for-21 for 137 yards and the two touchdowns, which gives him 30 TD passes for the year. That marks the third time in his career he's reached that plateau, and makes him and Miami's Dan Marino the only quarterbacks in NFL history to have three 30-touchdown seasons in their careers. Marino has four.

The second touchdown pass was vintage Favre impro-

visation. He avoided two potential sacks, covered at least 25 yards of the field scrambling back and forth, and found running back Dorsey Levens in the back of the end zone for a 5-yard score. That put the game away, 24-9.

His two interceptions, though, marked only the third time in 12 games that he failed to throw more touchdown passes than interceptions in a game.

"I was disappointed, as he was, with the interceptions in the red zone," Coach Mike Holmgren said. "He was trying so desperately to make plays that he was trying too hard."

Still, the spark for this Packers win came from the other side of the ball, via a missing ingredient in the past three weeks: Turnovers.

The Packers ended their streak of three games with-

Game 12 | PACKERS 24, RAMS 9

Rison's Presence, Play Lift Struggling Offense

BY CHRIS HAVEL
Press-Gazette

Andre Rison has a tattoo on his stomach that reads, "Only the strong survive."

The three-time Pro-Bowl receiver and newest member of the Packers believes the words are appropriate because he sees himself as strong and a survivor. On Sunday night, in his Packers debut, the man who began the week as "The NFL's Least Wanted Receiver" played true to his words.

Rison caught a team-high five passes for 44 yards to help the Packers capture a 24-9 victory over St. Louis on Sunday night in front of 61,499 at the Trans World Dome. It wasn't only Rison's presence in the lineup, but also his confident attitude, that impacted the Packers.

"He was like a rookie he was so excited," Packers coach Mike Holmgren said. "I took that into account and thought it might lead to some drops or mistakes, but it didn't. He was very solid and sound. I couldn't be more pleased with (Rison's) performance."

Rison's teammates credited him with providing some spark.

"Even if he doesn't catch a lot of passes, just the threat of him being on the field opened up a lot of options," tight end Keith Jackson said.

"It's scary," running back Edgar Bennett said. "And he doesn't even know all of the offense yet."

Rison said he knew about 40 plays and didn't break any patterns against the Rams.

"The week started out with me learning 10, then 15, then 20," he said. "The number of plays just kind of kept growing."

Brett Favre completed 25-of-37 passes for 192 yards and two touchdowns, his best game since a four-touchdown outing against Detroit three weeks ago. He looked more comfortable as the game wore on, completing 15-of-21 passes for 138 yards and both touchdowns in the second half.

Rookie Derrick Mayes was a junior high school star in Indianapolis when Rison was a rookie there with the Colts in 1989. He let Rison stay at his house when he arrived in Green Bay.

"He's a good roommate," Mayes said. "He doesn't give me any trouble."

Mayes said Rison's greatest impact was intangible.

"He put a lot of people's minds at ease," he said. "I'm still a rookie, so I have to keep a straight face about a lot of things, but (Rison) rubs off on people. He know how to have fun."

Rison, 29, was claimed on waivers Tuesday from Jacksonville, where he caught 34 passes in 11 starts before wearing out his welcome, in the opinion of Jaguars coach Tom Coughlin.

Rison said he had something to prove.

"I wanted to show people they were wrong who put this on me that I was undisciplined and ran bad routes and was a distraction to a team," Rison said. "Over the past several days, I've read every negative comment that someone could write about me. That hurts for me to see my children read things about me that aren't true. Tonight was a special night for me to play on national TV and for my kids to watch and for me to perform well. It was important for me to prove to people that I am one of the best receivers in the game. I've still got a lot of football ahead of me."

Rams linebacker Roman Phifer (58) and safety Toby Wright (32) double-team Packers fullback William Henderson.

out a takeaway by recovering two fumbles to go along with Evans' key interception.

One of the fumbles, a muffed snap by Banks that linebacker Brian Williams recovered, led to Favre's 6-yard touchdown pass to tight end Keith Jackson.

The other was equally important and prevented the first half from being a total disaster. It came on the free kick after Rams defensive end Kevin Carter caught Favre in the Packers' end zone and drew an intentional grounding penalty, resulting in an automatic safety.

That put the Rams ahead, 9-0, with 2:29 to play in the first half and gave them another shot at scoring because they presumably would get decent field position on the ensuing free kick. But Packers punter Craig Hentrich tried for extra hang time and hit the free punt unexpectedly short.

Rams return men Herman O'Berry and Jermaine Ross let the ball land between them, in the middle of a group of about five Rams players, and Packers safety Mike Prior caught the ball off one hop.

Chris Jacke later kicked a 37-yard field goal on the final play of the half to cut the lead to 9-3.

Packers	0	7	7	14	28
Bears	0	7	3	7	17

Packers Tame Bears

By Pete Dougherty
Press-Gazette

GREEN BAY, DEC. 1, 1996 — Dorsey Levens' biggest worries were unfounded.

Three months ago, when the Green Bay Packers demoted him to backup fullback just before the regular season started, he wondered whether they were phasing him out of their offense.

Thirteen weeks and 85 carries later, it's clear they weren't, and their reward came Sunday.

In their 28-17 win over the Chicago Bears on Sunday, Levens gave them a huge lift in a ball-control battle on sloppy Lambeau Field. He had the biggest rushing day of his three-year career, gaining all 69 of his yards in the second half as the Packers won back a ball-possession battle that the underdog Bears had dominated for the first 30 minutes.

"Your worst fear is to be on the bench," Levens said Sunday, recalling the day he found out that William Henderson had supplanted him as the starting fullback. "I like touching the ball, and when you're not on the field it makes it pretty much impossible to get your hands on the ball."

Levens' main contribution Sunday was running three times for 49 yards on a backbreaking drive in the fourth quarter that ended with his 10-yard run for a touchdown that put the Packers ahead, 21-10.

In the bigger picture, he also helped lift a rushing game that the Packers will need to win in the mud and ice and snow and cold of December and January at Lambeau Field. The Packers have two regular-season games left at Lambeau and hope to have two playoff games there as well.

Chicago, 5-8, came into this game on a roll defensively. The Bears had given up an average of only 13.6 points in their previous five games, and the most they had allowed in that stretch was 17 points to Denver, which was second in the NFL in scoring coming in the weekend.

Levens' second-half surge helped the Packers finish with 126 yards rushing, which is the first time in a month they've been over the 90-yard mark. Also, their 4.8 yards a carry was a season-high.

"We played against a good defensive team, so I feel a little bit better about how we're going on offense now," Coach Mike Holmgren said.

Holmgren certainly didn't feel that way, though, at the end of a first half that statistically was nothing short

Desmond Howard glides into the end zone after returning a punt 75 yards for a TD.

Game 13 | PACKERS 28, BEARS 17

of appalling.

The Bears, owners of the 25th-rated offense in the NFL, held the ball for nearly 22 of the first 30 minutes.

The Bears did it by pounding halfback Raymont Harris between the tackles again and again in hopes of running the clock, setting up the occasional play-action pass and keeping the Packers' offense off the field.

It worked for 30 minutes. Harris had 17 carries and 60 yards rushing at halftime, and the score was 7-7.

The Bears had trouble finishing their drives — their only score was a 15-yard touchdown pass from Dave Krieg to Bobby Engram. But they gashed the Packers' run defense enough to conjure memories of Kansas City's 27-20 win over Green Bay three weeks ago.

"The Kansas City game — Mike (Holmgren) will tell you the same thing — is about the only game in the three years I've been here where a team played more physical than we did," said Sean Jones, the Packers' right defensive end. "(The Bears) executed and ran their plays, but it wasn't like they were winning the physical battle."

The Packers turned things around completely in the second half. They gained 113 of their 126 yards rushing after intermission, with much of it coming on one-back alignments that kept the Bears from crowding the line of scrimmage.

Levens, who splits time with Edgar Bennett in the one-back offense, had only five carries. But three were for 15 yards or more, another was the 10-yard touchdown, and the fifth picked up a first down. His 24-yarder early in the fourth quarter was the Packers' longest rush of the season.

"Most of the time I touched the ball there was nobody in front of me," he said.

Sunday marked the first time in Levens' career he has led the Packers in rushing in a game — Bennett finished with 51 yards rushing on 16 carries. Levens nevertheless has been more of runner than a receiver

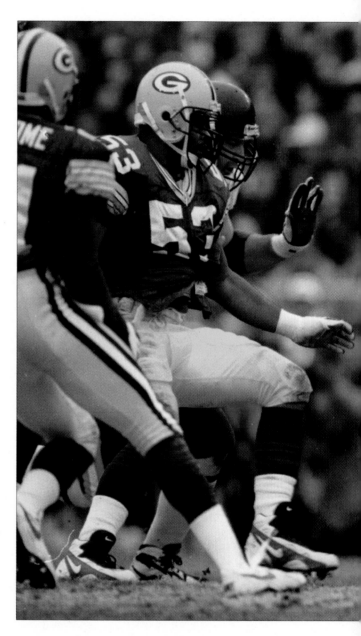

this year, which is a departure from last season.

As the starting fullback in '95 he was mainly a blocker and receiver. He finished fourth on the team in receptions (48) and had 36 rushes.

Now that Henderson is the primary fullback

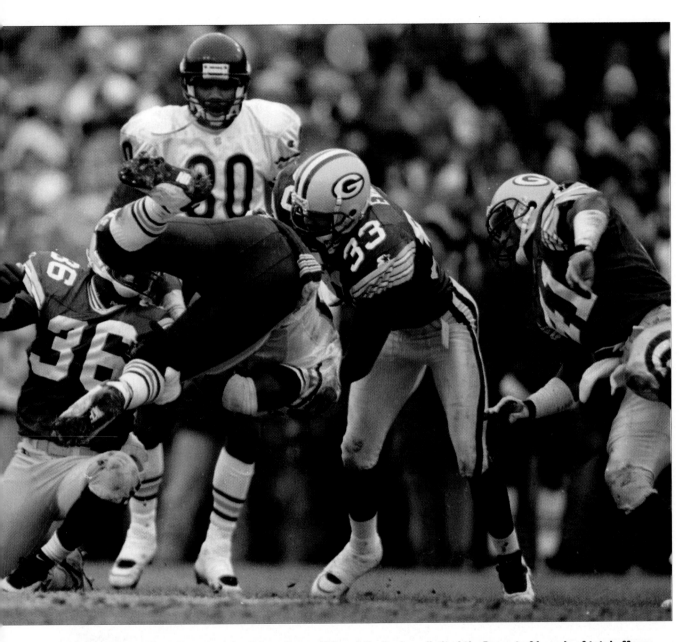

Safety LeRoy Butler (36), cornerback Doug Evans (33) and the Packers limited the Bears to 84 yards of total offense.

because of his lead-blocking skills, Levens has 85 rushes and only 25 receptions. He's had one game with no carries, at Minnesota, but also twice he's had more carries than Bennett: Against San Francisco, when he ran 10 times to Bennett's seven; and at Dallas, where he had nine carries to Bennett's eight.

Freeman, Supporting Cast Too Much For Bears

BY CHRIS HAVEL
Press-Gazette

All that Antonio Freeman needed to dominate the Chicago Bears' defense was his own talent and a strong supporting cast.

The most obvious member of that "cast" was the cumbersome white brace that protected the receiver's broken left forearm. It gave Freeman safe passage on his way to a career-high 10 catches for 156 yards.

Then there was Brett Favre, who showed supreme confidence in Freeman by throwing to him frequently, even though Freeman had missed five games.

And there was the Packers' strength and conditioning coaches who whipped Freeman into better shape during his five-week absence than he was before it.

Finally, there was the beleaguered Walt Harris. The Bears' rookie cornerback was back on his heels — and several steps behind Freeman's — throughout the Packers' 28-17 victory over the Bears in front of 59,682 at Lambeau Field.

"Free had an incredible performance," Packers defensive end Sean Jones said. "You've seen guys come back from injuries and contribute, but my goodness. To come back this game and dominate the way he did ... "

Coach Mike Holmgren was equally impressed.

"I think he had a great game for coming back and not playing," Holmgren said. "He caught a big one right in front of me and then he caught some good passes inside. It was good to have him back."

Freeman, a second-year receiver from Virginia Tech, said he fed off Favre's excitement regarding his return.

"(Favre) told me, 'We've got to have a coming-back party,' " Freeman said. "That's what we did. We came out and we were able to execute in the second half."

Actually, Freeman executed the entire game.

He caught five first-half passes for 101 yards, including a 41-yarder on his second reception. His most timely grab was a 30-yarder on a slant that helped to pull the Packers even at 7-7 right before halftime.

On the play, Freeman lined up wide left with Harris in single coverage. Freeman made it appear as if he were running an inside slant, which tempted Harris into jumping in front to make the interception. But Favre held onto the ball and then lofted a pass to Freeman, who had cut back outside.

The result was a Packers first down at the Bears' 19-yard line. On the next play, Favre hit Keith Jackson in the left corner of the end zone to set the stage for the second-half rout.

Freeman accepted little credit for his career day. Here is what he said about his "cast":

•On Favre: "The chemistry was there from the time I came back. We were running routes, I'd come out of my break, and the ball was right there."

•On the strength and conditioning coaches: "They kept my legs strong and kept me running when I wasn't able to practice. I was able to hit it full-tilt when I came back. I got back into sync."

•On the cast itself: "It didn't get in the way at all. I was used to it. I've been practicing the last two weeks with it. I was able to just let my natural abilities take control."

It appeared Freeman might be in for a tough day when he fumbled after his first reception. He caught a 14-yard pass over the middle, but was drilled by Bears

Marty Carter was one of the many Bears who couldn't catch Antonio Freeman, who had 10 catches for 156 yards.

safety Marty Carter, who forced the fumble.

After the game, Freeman said Carter's hit, and not the brace, caused the fumble.

"Actually, (Carter) hit me as I was trying to tuck the ball away," he said. "When you come back from an injury, you need that first hit to get going. After that first hit, I knew what I had to do and things went well from that point on."

Freeman's previous career day came at Chicago on Oct. 6, when he hauled in seven passes for 146 yards and two touchdowns. On Sunday, the Bears' secondary rolled its coverage toward Andre Rison and left Harris in single coverage with Freeman.

The results proved disastrous for the Bears.

Homemade Success

BY CHRIS HAVEL
Press-Gazette

A rugged man dressed in faded blue jeans and a motorcycle jacket hailed Mike Holmgren in the parking lot outside the Packers' headquarters at 1265 Lombardi Avenue.

He politely requested the head coach's autograph on this icy December day.

Without hesitation, Holmgren called a timeout in the midst of an interview, greeted the man with a hearty handshake and signed.

"Gotta take care of my guys," said Holmgren, a Harley-Davidson motorcycle enthusiast.

So it is with Holmgren.

Strip away his expertise regarding pro football's X's and O's. Remove his ability to properly evaluate talent. What remains is the underlying essence of Holmgren's success: He is an exceedingly decent person.

"My mom and dad raised us that way," he said. "In our family, you learned the golden rule. That's ingrained in us."

It is one of life's lessons that has served Holmgren well during his ascension to a place among the NFL's top coaches. It also is one reason he is a candidate to be named Coach of the Year.

"When the season started, we were picked to win everything," General Manager Ron Wolf said. "We also had the toughest schedule. (Holmgren) kept the team together and accomplished virtually all the goals set by the team. Today we have the best record in the

Coaching Resume

Mike Holmgren's coaching resume:

• Green Bay Packers: Head coach, 1992 to present. Regular season, 51-29; playoffs, 7-3.

• San Francisco 49ers: Offensive coordinator, 1989-91; quarterbacks coach 1986-88.

• BYU: Quarterbacks coach, 1982-85.

• San Francisco State: Offensive coordinator / quarterbacks coach, 1981.

NFC. That's impressive."

Indeed, the Packers, 12-3, have a chance to wrap up the NFC's home-field advantage today with a victory over Minnesota, 9-6, or a loss by fewer than 19 points, or a Carolina loss or tie at home against Pittsburgh.

A poll of 10 NFL writers late this week revealed seven votes for Carolina coach Dom Capers, whose 11-4 Panthers are closing in on the NFC's No. 2 seed

Near the end of the NFC title game against the Panthers, the Packers put their win — and Mike Holmgren — on ice.

and a first-round bye in the playoffs. Three writers named Denver coach Mike Shanahan as their choice for Coach of the Year.

Most cited Holmgren as an excellent candidate, but said his accomplishments were less stunning than Capers'.

"Heck, I think I'd probably vote for Dom, too," Holmgren said. "That's a remarkable thing that team has done. Now, I also think Mike (Shanahan) did a tremendous job. He had a hard row to hoe. I guess I'd vote for Dom though."

Holmgren, 48, said he won't be crestfallen if the award bypasses him this Christmas Eve. He tries to adhere to the same advice he gave his players when

the Pro Bowl balloting was announced.

There is a bigger prize to be won.

Besides, it wouldn't be the first time Coach of the Year honors eluded him. Nor is it likely to be the last. Where Holmgren is concerned, expectations are high, especially if quarterback Brett Favre remains healthy.

Building A Contender

Holmgren inherited a 4-12 team in 1992. He and Wolf whipped it into a 9-7 playoff contender that season. The following season they earned the team's first playoff berth in a non-strike year since 1972. They won a wild-card game at Detroit. The next season, they were home for a playoff game. Last year, they went 11-5 and managed a trip to the NFC championship game.

The progression has been steady.

"Everybody looks at it as 'Coach of that Year,'" said Bill Walsh, who hired Holmgren to coach the 49ers' quarterbacks in 1986. Walsh currently is a special assistant at San Francisco.

"But when you look at what Mike's done with the continuity of getting better and better — the guy's doing a fantastic job. To me, when a team keeps getting better, the coach should be recognized for it."

One of the secrets to Holmgren's success is how he manages his players. He can be warm and caring and he isn't afraid to show his sense of humor. But he also can be a strict disciplinarian when he deems its necessary.

"He has a really good sense of humor," 49ers quarterback Steve Young said. "For a football coach, he's very unusual. To me, that's a real compliment because so many times we get these stoic, non-people people coaching the ultimate people sport. If you're not good with people in football, then really you're 5 yards behind the line to start with."

Jim Fassel, the Arizona Cardinals' offensive coordinator, was Holmgren's roommate on road games during the University of Southern Cal's 1969 season.

Fassel, like Holmgren, was a quarterback . The two were vying for playing time. In fact, USC coach John McKay recruited Fassel from Fullerton College primarily because a knee injury jeopardized Holmgren's future.

"I've always liked Mike because when I transferred in he treated me like a friend," Fassel said. "He really didn't have to under the circumstances, but we hit it off and became friends. I'll always respect him for that."

Learning The Trade

Holmgren said much of his philosophy on how to treat players was spawned during his playing days at USC. His own playing career took him down many paths. He had been the highly recruited star. The talented player riding the bench because of a coach's decision. The injured afterthought.

Holmgren, who was named California's "Prep Athlete of the Year" in 1965, beat out Jim Plunkett for the award. He was recruited by Brigham Young, UCLA and USC.

"Mike Holmgren was the best high school quarterback I ever saw," said Dan Fouts, the San Diego Chargers' Hall of Fame quarterback.

Holmgren chose USC but rarely got an opportunity to play there. He sat behind Steve Sogge as a sophomore and junior, and behind Jimmy Jones as a senior. He completed 8 of 27 passes for 108 yards, one touchdown and one interceptions as a junior, despite playing on an injured knee.

Holmgren was ready to take over as the starting quarterback his senior year, but he badly damaged his left shoulder in a scrimmage the week before the season-opener against Nebraska.

"I'll never forget it," he said. "We had a full scrimmage and the quarterbacks were live. No red jerseys. I got tackled and came down on my shoulder and busted it up pretty good.

"That was the one that really hurt," he added, referring to the mental anguish of being sidelined, rather than physical pain. "I'd waited a long time to play. Then it didn't happen."

Injuries notwithstanding, Holmgren seemed destined for little playing time at USC. He was a prolific drop-back passer — "I could throw it around pretty good," he said — but the Trojans' system put a premium on mobility.

Between the injuries and John McKay's unwillingness to utilize Holmgren's strong arm, the opportunities were scarce.

"I was disappointed and angry for a long time," Holmgren said. "It took me a long time to get over that. But it's a great school. It's a tremendous school. I made lifelong friends. My only regret is I didn't get a chance to play more. Whether that would've led to a pro career, who knows?"

Holmgren did learn a valuable lesson.

"I have a lot of empathy for the guy that gets hurt," he said. "For the guy that doesn't get a chance to play. I think I really — you might get an argument from some of my players — but I think I've bent over backwards trying to be fair.

"At times growing up, I didn't think that happened. When I thought I wanted to get into coaching, which happened at a young age, these lessons in life came up. My parents approached it like this: 'Not everything is going to be fair, in your opinion, but that's life.

" 'Understand that. Learn from it. Build on it.' "

Overcoming Disappointment

Holmgren's rise from high school history teacher to head coach of the Packers was meteoric, but it had its share of disappointments along the way. Holmgren learned from those, too.

Three of the greater disappointments came after Holmgren's fourth season as Brigham Young's quarterbacks coach in 1985.

The first came when the University of Montana's head coaching job opened up. Holmgren pursued the job and was a finalist with Don Read.

"I really thought I had a chance to get it," Holmgren said. "It was my time to leave BYU."

Montana hired Read.

Said Holmgren, "I was really in the tank."

John Cooper, who currently coaches at Ohio State, became the head coach at Arizona State a few weeks later. Holmgren was interested in joining Cooper's staff at Arizona State. Holmgren, who had been recruited to UCLA by Cooper out of high school, asked BYU coach LaVell Edwards to make a call on

his behalf. Cooper liked Holmgren, but decided on Jim Colletto instead.

Finally, Holmgren was contacted by Lou Holtz, who'd been named head coach at Notre Dame. Holtz was in search of an offensive coordinator, or so he led Holmgren to believe. He interviewed Holmgren twice.

"I thought I had the job," Holmgren said. "I swear to this day, Holtz told me, 'You're the guy.' We were in New Orleans, so Jim and Cindy Lind and Kathy and I have this big celebration.

"When I get back to Utah, he tells me, 'I didn't do that. I'm not going to hire a coordinator.' "

Two weeks later, Walsh called and asked him to interview to be the 49ers' quarterback coach. Three weeks after the interview, Holmgren still hadn't heard anything. Then one day he was getting ready to go for a jog when a graduate assistant came running down the hallway.

Bill Walsh was on the telephone.

"I said, 'Yeah, right. Get out of here,' " Holmgren said. "But he goes, 'I'm not fooling. It's really him.' So I go flying back to my office. My secretary says, 'I told him you were jogging and he should call back.' "

Walsh did.

"He said, 'How would you like to work for us?' " said Holmgren. "I was trying to be really cool. I told him I had to talk it over with my wife."

For Holmgren, the missed opportunities led to the chance of a coaching lifetime with the 49ers. Three years after the University of Montana told Holmgren, "Thanks, but no thanks," he was being recruited by both the New York Jets and Arizona Cardinals.

Three years after that, he said "yes" to the Packers.

"I believe in how it works sometimes," he said. "I also believe this with all my heart. Wherever you are, be happy and work hard and continue to develop your expertise. Study. Learn. Become good at it. Then, when the time comes, you're ready."

What Makes Holmgren A Great Coach?

Here are explanations from those who know Packers coach Mike Holmgren:

BILL WALSH, *49ers special assistant:* "He's exceptionally bright. He is able to keep composure under real stress. He communicated with all groupings of athletes. He's got an outstanding football mind and he's a hands-on coach. Unless you are, generally you're at the mercy of everyone else. He has a real expertise in the passing game, among other things, that has served him well."

JIM FASSEL, *Arizona Cardinals offensive coordinator and Holmgren's roommate on road trips at USC:* "He has a great feel for the game. Knowledge is one thing. Anyone can be that. There aren't a lot of people at this level who aren't smart. But it takes a combination of a feel for the game and a feel for people. Mike's personality is such that you know where you stand with him. He commands respect, yet he's fun to be around. I would imagine his players really enjoy playing for him."

STEVE YOUNG, *49ers quarterback:* "He understands people. He can sit down and have a conversation with someone and know what kind of player he is. A lot of people measure it with objective things. Speed. How far you can jump. He's the kind of guy who measures it with subjective things. He can put together a team that's going to play hard. He knows the kind of personality he want his team to have and he demands it."

FRITZ SHURMUR, *Packers defensive coordinator:* "He has the three things you need to be a really good coach.

Mike Holmgren — an expert in the passing game.

He understands the X's and O's as well as anybody and he can teach it. He's also a very good manager of people. The thing that makes Mike unique is he combines those with the ability to evaluate talent. That's a rare thing when you've got all three of those attributes."

BOB HARLAN, *Packers president:* "Mike's ability as a communicator is extraordinary. He's also a good teacher, which is reflected in his background. He can be a close, warm friend to his players, but also a strict disciplinarian and he knows when to do each."

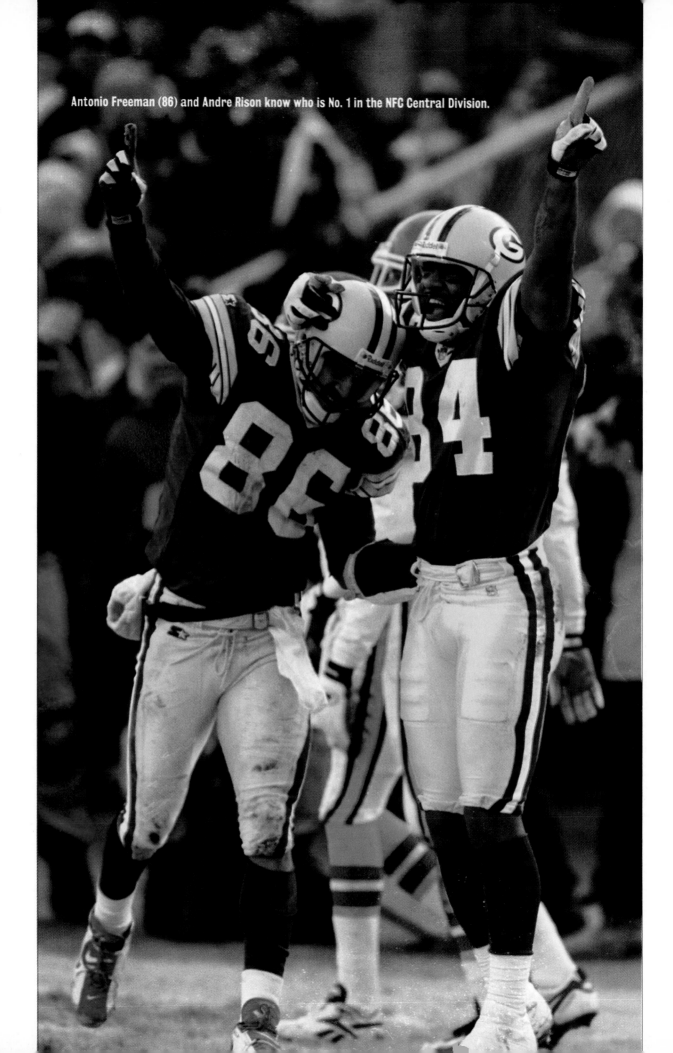

Antonio Freeman (86) and Andre Rison know who is No. 1 in the NFC Central Division.

Packers	3	10	7	21	41
Broncos	3	0	3	0	6

Central Title Clincher

By Pete Dougherty
Press-Gazette

Green Bay, Dec. 8, 1996 — Late in the second quarter, Brett Favre broke the huddle, surveyed the Denver Broncos' defense and called out "Chewy" as he headed toward the line of scrimmage.

Tight end Mark Chmura hadn't played in a month because of an arch injury, but he's been with Favre since 1992 and knew exactly what his quarterback meant: He was about to run a streak pattern, and Favre was telling him to look for the ball right away.

That is what they mean when they talk about chemistry between a quarterback and his receiver. The chemistry the Packers lacked when Chmura and starting receivers Robert Brooks and Antonio Freeman were all out with injuries three long weeks ago.

The result: Chmura caught the pass, rumbled through two tackles and picked up 29 yards. The play set up the Packers' first touchdown, gave them a 10-point lead going into halftime and sparked a second-half onslaught in which they clinched their second straight NFC Central Division title with a 41-6 win over the Broncos on Sunday at Lambeau Field.

"That's what playing together for five years does," Chmura said. "We're on the same page. We probably share the same brain."

The Broncos were severely crippled without injured quarterback John Elway and lacked a sense of urgency because they already have sewn up home-field advantage for the AFC playoffs. Nevertheless, they came into this game with the NFL's third-rated defense for yards allowed and fourth-rated for points given up.

But after a stodgy first half in which the Packers led, 6-3, until that first touchdown with 17 seconds left in the second quarter, the Packers cut through that highly rated defense for 204 yards and four touchdowns in the second half.

Buoyed by Chmura's return from a partially torn arch, the Packers now have all their offensive weapons in place except for Brooks, who is out for the year because of a knee injury.

"You can see what having all these weapons can mean to this offense and to Brett's confidence," Chmura said.

Though it was not a vintage Favre performance, he finished 20-for-38 for 280 yards and four TD's.

For the first time in a month, he had the potent tight end duo of Chmura and Keith Jackson as part of his offensive mix, and Coach Mike Holmgren deployed it regularly. Chmura finished with four receptions for 70 yards, and Jackson had three receptions, including one touchdown. But receiver Antonio Freeman probably was the main beneficiary on this day with his second big game in a row since returning from a broken

Game 14 | PACKERS 41, BRONCOS 6

Packers quarterback Brett Favre was 20-of-38 passing for 280 yards and four TD's against Denver.

left forearm.

Last week against Chicago he set personal highs for receptions (10) and receiving yards (156). He followed that up against the Broncos with another personal best for receiving yards (175) on nine receptions. Among his catches were three touchdowns, including a slant that he turned into a 51-yard scoring play by breaking a tackle by cornerback Tory James.

"When we went with two tight ends, especially when we were (lined up) on the same side, we got a lot of attention over there," Jackson said. "We tried to throw a pass over there early and they had four guys trying to cover two. That helps out the guys on the weak side."

It probably hasn't hurt Freeman that Andre Rison is the Packers' starting flanker, either. Rison caught only one pass Sunday, and it's clear he still hasn't developed good timing with Favre. But his playmaking potential demands attention.

"(Rison) has the same presence on the field as Robert Brooks has," Freeman said. "We have Chmura back, Jackson, now we're lined up across the board. I think this offense is getting that feeling back again."

Freeman has managed to catch 19 passes for 331 yards in the past two games despite the bulky cast protecting his left forearm that he'll wear the rest of the season. He did juggle one pass Sunday that he didn't corral until he was out of bounds, but besides that didn't miss a catchable ball. In fact, he had more drops before he was hurt and says the cast has improved his concentration.

"A lot of times I tend to body catch, I let the ball get to my body, that's what causes a lot of those problems," he said. "And when you get those easy balls sometimes you tend to relax and lose your concentration."

Now that Chmura is back, Jackson goes back from an every-down player to splitting time again at tight

Santana Dotson (71) watches as Packer teammate LeRoy Butler wraps up Broncos quarterback Bill Musgrave.

end. That might change his mind-set — "Now I go back to instant offense, like a sixth-man (in basketball)," he said — but won't necessarily curb his production.

In two of three games Chmura missed, Jackson caught three passes, which was his reception total Sunday against the Broncos. He's played the bulk of the season as Chmura's backup, yet is a leading candidate to make the Pro Bowl, especially after adding a 1-yard touchdown catch Sunday that gives him nine for the year.

Dallas' Eric Bjornson leads the NFC's tight ends in receptions with 47. Jackson has only 37, but his average per catch is significantly higher (11.8 to 8.1), and his nine touchdown receptions led the NFC as of Sunday evening.

"(Jackson) better make it," Chmura said. "I think there's no question that he does deserve it. He's got my vote."

Said Jackson: "I'd love to go to the Pro Bowl, but I'd rather win a Super Bowl more than anything."

Packers Know They Aren't Done Yet

BY CHRIS HAVEL
Press-Gazette

The Packers reacted to Sunday's busting of the Broncos in proper fashion, which is to say they did as much shrugging as celebrating.

They showed class and restraint while accepting the second straight NFC Central championship that came with their 41-6 victory over Denver. They didn't parade around Lambeau Field or carry on in the locker room. They saved the hokey Gatorade dous-

Reggie White responds to the cheers from the Packer fans at Lambeau Field.

ing for a more appropriate place, such as New Orleans.

They even acknowledged John Elway's absence likely made a difference.

"Yeah," safety LeRoy Butler said. "Maybe the score would've been something like 40-27. He's probably good for 14."

The Packers, 11-3, know the NFC's home-field advantage is the greater goal. Anything less would be as disappointing as a Cowboys' drug rehab program.

Jim McMahon summed up Green Bay's position.

"We haven't accomplished (blank) yet," he said. "We're in the big dance, but that's about it."

Sean Jones echoed the sentiment.

"Starting the season the way we did, this (division title) was a foregone conclusion. If we hadn't won the thing, it would've been a bigger collapse than Houston-Buffalo," said Jones, referring to the Bills' 1991 playoff comeback from a 32-point deficit against the Oilers.

Still, it is both necessary and proper to thank the many folks who helped make the Packers' back-to-back NFC Central titles possible.

First, there is the Packers' rope-a-dope offense. It lulls defenses to sleep, then it strikes. It wheezes like a chain smoker with pneumonia for one half, than takes off like a well-oiled Lamborghini the next.

The Packers have scored 70 second-half points in the past three games, which is more than they scored in the preceding four games (67) combined. Next time they win the toss, the should elect to skip the first two quarters.

There is Brett Favre, the only NFL quarterback capable of throwing for four touchdowns on his worst day.

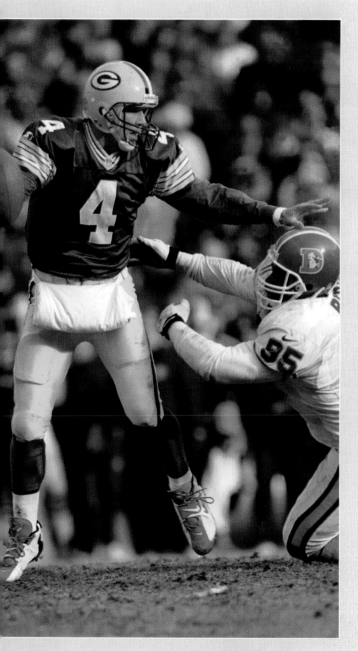

Quarterback Brett Favre skips out of the reach of Broncos defensive tackle Michael Dean Perry.

"He still goes brain-dead every once in awhile," McMahon said. "I don't think it'll change. Not when you've got confidence in yourself like he does."

There is Antonio Freeman, who changes casts the way Superman changes capes. At this rate, he might have to consider wearing casts on both arms.

There is the swarming defense. It made Terrell Davis look like a sixth-round draft pick and Shannon Sharpe look like Sterling's adopted brother.

There is Butler's timely blitzing and, just as important, a secondary that can maintain decent coverage when he doesn't get to the quarterback.

There is John Elway's left hamstring, Bill Musgrave's right arm and Coach Mike Shanahan's heady decision to tailor a game play bearing the inscription "Discretion is the better part of valor."

There is the Vikings and Lions and Bears and Bucs, four-of-a-kind who round out the NFC Central by adding up to one big zero. If this were a city softball league, they'd all have to drop down a division next season.

There are the 60,712 fans who showed up at Lambeau Field in 9-degree wind chill.

There is Dorsey Levens, who puts the "run" in running attack. He churned out a career-high 86 yards against the NFL's No. 1 rushing defense, proving that last week's 69-yard effort was just a warmup.

There is the classy Edgar Bennett, who had more attempts (nine) than yards (5) on Sunday, and still managed to smile at the Packers' victory.

There is defense coordinator Fritz Shurmur, one old dog who continues to teach the rest of the league new tricks.

Ultimately, there is Coach Mike Holmgren, who manages to keep his team from getting too full of itself too soon.

Packers	3	7	6	15	31
Lions	0	0	3	0	3

Howard Sparks Pack

By Pete Dougherty
Press-Gazette

PONTIAC, DEC. 15, 1996 — Desmond Howard turned the punt return into the Green Bay Packers' best offensive weapon Sunday.

On a day when the Packers sputtered early, he set a team record of 167 yards in punt returns, including the key play — a 92-yarder for a touchdown in the second quarter.

That play not only got him a personal milestone — the NFL record for punt-return yardage in a season — it also was a tension-breaking first touchdown that sparked the Packers to a 31-3 trouncing of the Detroit Lions at the Pontiac Silverdome.

"Coming to the finish line, when you're supposed to beat a team, that's when you sometimes struggle a little more," said tight end Keith Jackson. "You need somebody to make a big play, and he did it."

With the win, the Packers clinched a first-round bye in the playoffs and put themselves in prime position for home-field advantage for the entire NFC playoffs. The only way they can lose the home field is if the Minnesota Vikings beat them by more than 18 points this week at Lambeau Field, where the Packers have won 15 straight games, including the playoffs.

Sunday was the culmination of a watershed season for Howard. It was suggested he has resurrected his NFL career in a Packers uniform.

"Resurrect means something died," he said. "Noth-ing ever died in me."

Perhaps, but just five months ago, the once coveted Heisman Trophy winner — Washington selected him fourth overall in the 1992 draft — was on the NFL scrap heap. The Packers didn't even have to pay him a signing bonus to get him to agree to a $300,000 contract for this season.

At age 26, he has reestablished himself as a valuable commodity by becoming one of the many weapons in the NFL's highest-scoring offense. As the Packers' punt returner, he has been both durable and productive, with his 791 yards in punt returns — breaking the NFL record of 692 set by the Raiders' Fulton Walker in 1985.

"This season has been huge," said Packers receiver Don Beebe. "This year will carry him for a few more years. If he's not in Green Bay (next season) he'll be somewhere. He's the best punt returner in the league."

Howard's gaudy 33.4-yard average per return Sunday was mainly because of the 92-yarder, but on his other four returns he averaged 18 yards. Among them

Desmond Howard races past the Lions on his way to a 92-yard punt return for a touchdown in the second quarter.

was a 22-yarder that set up the Packers' first field goal, and a 34-yarder that put them in Detroit territory, though the possession ended when quarterback Brett Favre was intercepted in the end zone.

"He's very quick, he catches the ball extremely easily and he has great vision," said Nolan Cromwell, the Packers' special-teams coach. "He knows who the

unblocked people are that he had to make miss."

The key play, though, was the 92-yard touchdown.

The Packers have been slow starters on offense in recent weeks, and on Sunday they gained 36 total yards in two first-quarter possessions.

Howard already had given them a boost with his first return — the 22-yarder that set up Chris Jacke's

Game 15 | PACKERS 31, LIONS 3

kick. On his second return, he picked up several key blocks that helped him go all the way.

The first was by Beebe just after Howard had caught the ball at his own 8. Beebe never had played or even practiced as a blocker on the outside flyers, but injuries to back-up safeties Roderick Mullen and Michael Robinson landed him the duty Sunday. On his second opportunity, after Detroit's Jocelyn Borgella finally had fought through blocking partner Terry Mickens, Beebe picked him off just as he was closing in Howard.

That gave Howard an unmolested start toward an alley on the right side of the field. Then, about 15 yards downfield, he broke a tackle and got a key block from Calvin Jones. That allowed him to cut back to his left, and he had only to outrun punter Mark Royals to give the Packers a 10-0 lead.

It was Howard's third punt return for a touchdown this season, which leaves him one game to tie the NFL record of four, set by Detroit's Jack Christiansen in 1951 and tied by Denver's Rick Upchurch in 1976.

"(Howard) is special because he sets up his blocks," Jackson said. "He's one of those guys like Mel Gray who not only set up the guy in front of them, but he also sets up guys two or three people away. That's unique and hard to find, and I'm glad we've got him."

The 10-0 lead held up until halftime, and Favre threw for 157 yards as the Packers put away the Lions with three second-half touchdowns.

Howard still has another week to add to his record-setting season. He has a higher average (14.6 yards a return) than Walker (11.2) did in '85 and has managed to get through the year without injury.

"If I still was in Washington, I'd be behind Brian Mitchell, who's going to his second-straight Pro Bowl (as a return man)," Howard said. "Then they'd be questioning everything because they'd never see what I can do. Now I have the opportunity to do something special."

Packers Assemble Dynamite Defense

By Chris Havel
Press-Gazette

Ron Wolf arrived in Green Bay with two priorities.

Get a quarterback. Build a defense.

The Packers' GM achieved the first by bamboozling the Falcons into thinking their third-string quarterback for his first-round draft pick was a sweet deal.

The second, and occasionally overlooked part of the Packers' renaissance, took considerably more time, money and energy to create. That's the way it is with championship defenses. They aren't won in lotteries or dice games. They can't be bought or stolen. They are developed. Forged. Molded.

They bear the label "A ton of assembly required."

But when it comes together, as the Packers' defense did in Sunday's 31-3 taming of the Lions, it can tear even the most talented of offenses apart.

From start to finish, the Lions' offense was as non-threatening as Scott Mitchell's intended receiver. It was as irrelevant as the majority of his passes, most of which were neither here nor there.

The Packers are 12-3 thanks to Desmond Howard's feet, the punt return team's conscientiousness and last, but not least, the defense's domination. The Packers have surrendered 18 touchdowns in 15 games, including none for eight straight quarters.

Fritz Shurmur, the crusty and crafty architect behind it all, felt compelled to blow his defense's

Lions quarterback Scott Mitchell feels the strain of an afternoon of being chased by Packers end Reggie White.

horn after the game. No problem, Fritz. Here's a tuba.

"It was a magnificent effort today," he said. "We had to control the run but also, with as many threats as they have, to stop them in the passing game. That was a magnificent effort ... on turf."

Reggie White set the tone by making Lions right tackle Scott Conover look like a rag doll. When starter Zefross Moss went out with a knee injury in the first quarter, the Lions threw Conover to the Christian. White ate him alive.

Edgar Bennett was too much for the Vikings to handle, rushing for 109 yards and one touchdown on 18 carries.

Packers	7	3	14	14	38
Vikings	7	3	0	0	10

A Record Win

By Pete Dougherty
Press-Gazette

GREEN BAY, DEC. 22, 1996 — It was the perfect playoff precursor.

With a 38-10 win over the Minnesota Vikings in the regular-season finale Sunday, the Green Bay Packers handily clinched the home-field advantage in the NFC and dominated like they haven't since the first half of the year, before midseason injuries took some of the punch from their offense.

They displayed excellence in all phases of the game in capping a season in which they set an NFL record for fewest touchdowns allowed in a 16-game season (19); an NFC record for touchdown (39 by Brett Favre); and an NFL record for punt-return yardage (875 by Desmond Howard).

At 13-3, tied with Denver for best record in the NFL, they now go into their bye week on a high as they prepare for the single-elimination games that ultimately will be the measure of their 1996 season.

"Desmond did a fantastic job of getting us field position," receiver Antonio Freeman said. "The defense slowed them up and kept them from scoring. The offense systematically went down the field, and everybody got some touches. That's the way you'd write it in a storybook."

Though the Packers enter the playoffs on a five-game winning streak and are savoring the home-field advantage they have earned, they nevertheless face a potential gauntlet to get to the Super Bowl. With the

way the seedings have fallen, they very well could have to beat San Francisco and Dallas back-to-back to get to their first NFL championship game since Super Bowl II in 1968.

The 49ers and Cowboys, though no longer the dominant teams in the regular season, have combined to win the last four Super Bowls and six of the last eight. The Packers lost to the Cowboys earlier this season and beat the 49ers in overtime at home.

"The thing about it is, we have a week off. It's nice to have the week to rest," tight end Keith Jackson said. "If you want to be king of the hill, you have to beat the kings, and (the Cowboys and 49ers) are the kings. What better way is there to go out than to beat the kings?"

Said defensive tackle Santana Dotson: "It doesn't matter to me. We have goals, and whoever comes to town stands in the way of our goals."

Of all the marks the Packers set Sunday, the most impressive reflects that they truly are a complete team.

Game 16 | Packers 38, Vikings 10

They not only finished the season with the most points scored in the league (456), they gave up the fewest point (210) as well.

The last team to lead the NFL in both categories was the 1972 Miami Dolphins, the only team in league history to go unbeaten and untied through an entire season.

"If's fun for two days or so," defensive end Sean Jones said of the milestones the Packers reached Sunday. "But the next three weeks will tell how great this team is."

The Packers finished with one of their most impressive offensive games of the year against a Vikings team that had limited them to 60 yards rushing and sacked Favre seven times in the first meeting.

For one, the Packers rushed for a season-high 233

Keith Jackson catches a 23-yard TD pass from Brett Favre — and a high five from Andre Rison — in the fourth quarter.

yards, which is the most they've run for since the 257 they gained against Chicago in 1994. Running back Edgar Bennett's 109 yards was their first 100-yard game of the season.

Favre didn't have a huge day (15-for-23, 202 yards) but he averaged 13.5 yards a completion and threw three touchdown passes. That gives him the third-most (39 this year) and fourth-most (38 last year) touchdown passes in a season in NFL history. Miami's Dan Marino holds the top two spots with 48 in 1984 and 44 in '86.

Receiver Andre Rison also finally became a factor, in the second half Sunday, catching three passes for 46 yards in the third quarter. Included was his first touchdown since joining the Packers for their final five games, a sliding 2-yarder for a touchdown that put them ahead, 24-10. Rison, their starting flanker, had only five receptions in the previous three games combined.

And Howard continued to shine as a return man. Among his four punt returns were a 47-yarder and 25-yarder that set up touchdowns, and he brought back his one kickoff return for 40 yards.

"Rison's catching the ball," said Tom Lovat, the Packers' offensive line coach. "Our two (running) backs are humming. You have Desmond Howard, he's going to get you field position. People have to be a little concerned when they play the Green Bay Packers."

The Packers also got the satisfaction of blowing out the Vikings, who have become their biggest NFC Central Division rival in the Mike Holmgren-Ron Wolf era. Minnesota provided one of the few low points of the Packers' season when it beat them, 30-21, in Minneapolis in the fourth week, and rubbed it in with trash talking during and after that game.

Early Sunday, the animosity between the teams was evident in several small scuffles and extra hitting at the end of plays. The ugliest moment came when Vikings

The Packers skinned the Vikings, giving their frozen fans at Lambeau Field high hopes for the postseason.

defensive back Corey Fuller intentionally poked Packers center Frank Winters in the eye after Winters had thrown a block at the end of a play on the Packers' first drive.

"We wanted to hit hard and hit hard all day," Dotson said. "It was one of those street fight kind of games."

Said Vikings linebacker Jeff Brady: "They've been waiting all year to get us back up here."

Talk Is Cheap, Just Like The Vikings

BY CHRIS HAVEL
Press-Gazette

The Packers and their fans took great delight Sunday in one of the most effective recycling efforts in Green Bay history.

It went like this: The Vikings talked trash. The Packers made them eat their words.

When it was all over but the burping, the Packers had a 38-10 victory and a month's worth of momentum heading into their NFC divisional playoff game.

The Vikings? They were reminded that jawing and yapping isn't a suitable replacement for blocking and tackling. Whether they learned their lesson is debatable. Packers safety LeRoy Butler tried to silence them with logic.

"I told them to look at the scoreboard," he said.

The advice fell on deaf ears. Minnesota should've known better than to rile up the home team.

As if the slick sod, blustery wind and fire-breathing fans weren't bad enough, the Vikings' pea-brained linebacker, Jeff Brady, decided to pop off after last week's victory against Tampa Bay.

Brady, whom the Vikings picked up after the Packers set him out on the curb a few years back, said he planned to go head-hunting Sunday. But as Edgar Bennett proved repeatedly, you can't hit what you can't catch. Nor can you hit what you can't touch, a situation created by Green Bay's offensive line.

Brady was in on four tackles, fewer than either of the Vikings' safeties.

Sean Jones slips past Todd Steussie (73) and wraps up Brad Johnson in the second quarter.

Cornerback Corey Fuller's eye-gouging of center Frank Winters was the dirtiest stunt in professional sports since Andrew Golota decided to turn Riddick Bowe's groin into his private punching bag.

At least Bowe's groin was protected.

After the game, Winters' left eye was red where the blood had seeped into the corners. His sight was blurred much of the game. He had double-vision, too, but still picked the correct Vikings to knock backward.

"It was a cheap shot. It was blatant," Winters said.

After the game, Brady said he didn't regret supplying the Packers with enough bulletin board material to fill a warehouse wall. Other than that, Brady didn't have much to say about anything.

On this day, talk — like the Vikings — was cheap.

Packers quarterback Brett Favre delivers a perfect pass against Chicago on Dec. 1.

Brett Favre | OFFENSIVE LEADER

Encore Performance

By CHRIS HAVEL
Press-Gazette

GREEN BAY, DEC. 30, 1996 — Brett Favre has joined NFL legends Jim Brown, Johnny Unitas and Joe Montana, plus the 49ers' Steve Young, as the only two-time Most Valuable Players in league history.

Does the Packers' quarterback belong in such lofty company? Hall of Fame coach Bill Walsh, now special assistant with the 49ers, said, "absolutely."

"You can't be the MVP twice without being right at the very top, and one of the very best, to ever play," he said. "There is no question he has become one of the three or four premier quarterbacks in the game. And there are those who would say he is the best."

Favre received 52 or 93 ballots by a nationwide panel of sports writers in voting announced by The Associated Press. He and Montana (1989 and '90) are the only players in league history to win consecutive MVP awards.

Favre, 27, threw for an NFC-record 39 touchdowns while leading the Packers, 13-3, to a second straight NFC Central Division title.

Sherman Lewis, the Packers' offensive coordinator, said Favre's second MVP season was more impressive than the first.

"He's a very strong individual," Lewis said. "With all the doubt that was circulating before the season as to how he would handle the pressure, to have the year he had is outstanding."

Favre's offseason troubles have been well documented.

He spent 46 days at the Menninger Clinic in Tope-

MVP Numbers

Listed below is a statistical breakdown of Brett Favre's MVP seasons.

	1995	1996
Attempts	570	543
Completions	359	325
Yards	4,413	3,899
Completion pct.	63.0	59.9
Touchdowns	38	39
Interceptions	13	13
Longest completion	99	80
Rating	99.5	95.8

ka, Kan., this past offseason to receive treatment for an addiction to the painkiller Vicodin. His 19-year-old sister, Brandi, was arrested in connection with a drive-by shooting in Slidell, La. His 29-year- old brother, Scott, was arrested on felony drunk driving charges after a July 20 crash that killed a close family friend.

Favre responded by throwing himself into his work.

He arrived at training camp in excellent shape and vowed to win a Super Bowl. Then he backed it up by

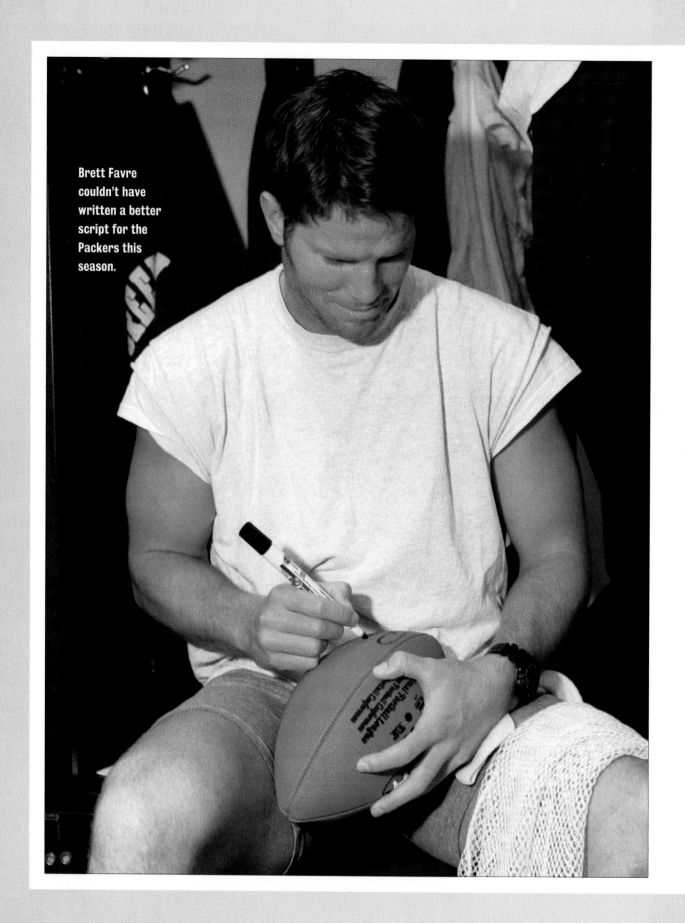

Brett Favre couldn't have written a better script for the Packers this season.

leading the Packers to an 8-1 start.

Tight end Mark Chmura, who is a close friend of Favre's, wasn't surprised.

"I just know he's a fighter and he loves it when people lose faith in him," Chmura said. "It drives him even more."

Injuries to go-to receiver Robert Brooks, talented split end Antonio Freeman and Chmura caused the offense to sputter at midseason. Left tackle Ken Ruettgers' bad knees and eventual retirement didn't help.

Favre was sacked a career-high 40 times. The young quarterback could have grumbled and pointed fingers.

Instead, he tried to instill confidence in a receiving corps that included newcomers Don Beebe, Andre Rison, Desmond Howard and Derrick Mayes.

"Brett played a big role in holding it together by showing confidence in the guys," Lewis said. "He went out of his way to show he trusted them. He went to them and he wasn't scared to throw to any of them."

The results were impressive. Beebe responded by catching a career-high 11 passes for 220 yards and a touchdown in the Packers' 23-20 overtime victory against the 49ers.

"It was like, 'OK, if it wasn't tough enough on me to start the season, let's make it a little tougher,'" Favre said. "We'll take Robert out. Ruettgers is not going to be back, and that's the most important position on the offense — left tackle. And then along the way, we'll take your No. 2 receiver. It was like, 'OK we'll put you to the test and see how you respond.'

"I'd much rather have Robert and Antonio and Ruettgers and all these guys to go to battle with, but it's not going to be that way all the time. I think I responded well to it, to any type of adversity, because I've had a bunch this year."

Packers quarterbacks coach Marty Mornhinweg said he and Favre shared the joy of a second straight MVP award in typical fashion.

Brett Favre hugs quarterbacks coach Marty Mornhinweg after the Monday night win over Niners.

"We high-fived," he said.

Mornhinweg, who replaced Steve Mariucci, said Favre made what might have been an awkward situation a snap. Mariucci, who left to become the head coach at the University of California, had a close relationship with Favre.

"Brett's attitude made (the adjustment) easy," Mornhinweg said. "It's been great. His main goal is to win the Super Bowl and that's what everyone on the team is after, so that makes it pretty easy.

"There are so many variables that go into having a super year like he did. Certainly, his play is the most important."

Walsh said Favre's spontaneity sets him apart from the NFL's rank-and-file.

"All three (Young, Montana and Favre) can make spontaneous plays that only they can make," he said. "Combine that with an outstanding system that provides a platform from which they can thrive, a strong supporting case and excellent coaching, and it adds up to something special."

Packers safety LeRoy Butler stretched his potential during the 1996 season and wound up back on the All-Pro team.

Butler Back On All-Pro Team, Joining Favre

By Pete Dougherty
Press-Gazette

Green Bay, Dec. 23, 1996 — Early last spring, Barry Rubin began visiting LeRoy Butler in Florida every six weeks or so for customized off-season workouts.

Rubin, the Packers' strength and conditioning assis-

tant, would stay in Butler's home town of Jacksonville for three or four days at a time, putting the Packers' strong safety through workouts that emphasized improving flexibility.

He came at Butler's request, and Butler insists this began before General Manager Ron Wolf said at the team's stockholders' meeting that Butler needed to improve his conditioning to get back to his Pro Bowl

Brett Favre | OFFENSIVE LEADER

and All-Pro form of 1993.

The result? While continuing to adhere to Rubin's program during the 1996 season, and with a special diet designed by strength coach Kent Johnston, Butler, at age 28, is back playing at peak form. He not only was voted to the Pro Bowl this season after a two-year absence, he's also received a more prestigious honor — being named to The Associated Press' All-Pro team as one of the two best safeties in the NFL.

"I don't feel like I would be close (to playing this well) without those guys," Butler said of Johnston and Rubin. "In fact, I know I wouldn't. I'd be just another average player who thinks he can get it done with his natural ability."

Butler is joined on the first team by one Packers teammate, quarterback Brett Favre, who was voted to The AP's first team for the second straight season.

A panel of sports reporters — three from each NFL city and several national at-large voters, as well — choose The AP's All-Pro team.

Butler made it on the strength of his personal accomplishments, combined with the increased publicity the Packers had this year as they tied with Denver for the best record in the NFL at 13-3.

Fritz Shurmur, the Packers' defensive coordinator, lined up Butler all over the field to take advantage of his abilities both as a cover man and blitzer. Butler finished with 6½ sacks, which is one sack short of setting the NFL record for a defensive back, and he had five interceptions. He also was second on the team with 88 tackles, tied for second on the team with 14 passes defensed, and he forced one fumble and recovered one fumble.

"Everybody wants to make the Pro Bowl, but All-Pro ... it becomes like your last name: LeRoy Butler, All-Pro," Butler said. "But I couldn't have done it without the team doing well and without my strength and conditioning coaches and my secondary coach

(Bob Valesente)."

Butler said the improved flexibility he's gained since last spring has been the biggest factor in his return to national prominence. About twice a week, Rubin puts him through a half-hour stretching routine that has made him more flexible and thus faster and less injury prone.

"When (Rubin) came down, he just pushed LeRoy," said Packers halfback Edgar Bennett, who also lives in Jacksonville and who played in college with Butler at Florida State. "I'm sure on some days when LeRoy wanted to play golf, (Rubin) would say, 'Let's workout first and then play golf.'"

Butler said his worst game this season was at Kansas City, when he had been sick and had to skip his stretching workouts that week. Then, two weeks later, he had one of his best games of the year against St. Louis with six tackles, including two sacks, after he had fully regained his flexibility.

"I've had no injuries, and I'm a lot looser," he said. "I feel like Nadia Comaneci with all the stretching I do."

Being selected to the All-Pro team this year was especially gratifying for Favre because of a difficult offseason, during which he spent six weeks in a rehabilitation clinic for an addiction to painkillers.

"Even though a lot of people had predicted us to scale new heights, I think there were a lot a skeptics out there, too, saying, 'I think a lot of it is false predictions,'" Favre said. "So it was like we had something to prove.

"I said going into this season that winning All-Pro and winning MVP and all these things is flattering, but it's more of a challenge to come back and do it again. Because everybody wants to know is this guy for real? Or is he a one-year wonder?"

Favre's 39 TD passes this year led the NFL. It was the third highest single-season total in NFL history.

Defensive end Reggie White was the only Packer voted to The AP's second team.

Packers	14	7	7	7	35
49ers	0	7	7	0	14

One Down, Two To Go

By Pete Dougherty
Press-Gazette

GREEN BAY, JAN. 4, 1997 — Is it even possible to overestimate just what Lambeau Field means to these Green Bay Packers?

They've now won 17 straight there, the most recent being Saturday's humbling of the San Francisco 49ers, 35-14, in an NFC divisional playoff game.

No wonder the Packers so desperately wanted, even needed, the home-field advantage throughout the play-offs. They've seen each of their last three seasons end at Texas Stadium, and their most recent disappointment there, a 21-6 loss in November, drove home the importance of facing the Cowboys in Green Bay.

Now they might get the chance, though Dallas today first must defeat the Carolina Panthers in Charlotte, N.C., which no team has done this year.

No matter the outcome, though, the winner has to go through Lambeau to get to the Super Bowl. The vanquished 49ers can testify to the difficulty of that task.

"Good luck," said 49ers receivers Jerry Rice to the Cowboys or Panthers. "It's going to be tough. When (the Packers) are running the ball and throwing the ball

Mike Prior (top) and his teammates caused three San Francisco fumbles, and the Packers recovered two of them.

Sean Jones & Co. are headed in the right direction.

like they are, and they've got Brett Favre back there, it's not going to be easy for anybody to beat them."

It's difficult to imagine Green Bay not relishing the chance to play the Cowboys at home after losing to them in Dallas seven straight times the past three-plus seasons. Many Packers fans showed their preferred opponent by chanting, "We want Dallas" in the final five minutes of Saturday's win.

But Coach Mike Holmgren took a preventive strike against his players overemphasizing revenge on the Cowboys by establishing the team's mind-set immediately after it had dispatched the 49ers. To a man after Saturday's win, the Packers' theme was that they don't care who they play.

"We don't care about Dallas," receiver Antonio Freeman said. "We want whoever wins that game (today)."

Said defensive end Sean Jones: "That's what happened to San Francisco, they wanted us so bad. Be careful what you wish for."

In advancing to the NFC championship game, the Packers clearly were the better team and might have had a shutout if not for two special-teams miscues that set up the 49ers' touchdowns.

Overall, Green Bay prevailed in all the crucial phases and at all the critical junctures of the game.

The Packers pounced early with the invaluable Desmond Howard's game-breaking punt returning. He took the 49ers' opening-drive punt for a 71-yard touchdown, and their third punt 46 yards to San Francisco's 7, setting up a 14-0 Packers lead.

"He took them right out of the game when he took their initial punt for a touchdown," General Manager Ron Wolf said. "The next time he touches the ball we go in again. It's 14-0 and we've got 9 yards in total offense."

Then when the 49ers put some doubt in the game's outcome by scoring back-to-back touchdowns off

Packers defensive lineman Gilbert Brown slams into Niners running back Tommy Vardell at the line of scrimmage.

turnovers to cut the lead to 21-14, the Packers slammed the door. They made their first possession of the second half the game-determining possession by hammering 11 runs out of 13 plays on a 72-yard drive that pushed the lead back to two touchdowns.

"We didn't want this game to slip away," tight end Mark Chmura said. "(The giveaways) fired us up offensively. We said, 'Enough is enough. Let's get it done.' "

They also accomplished what they had failed to do in the first meeting this season with the 49ers — run the ball.

Back in their 23-20 overtime win over San Francisco in mid-October, the Packers rushed for only 68 yards and 2.6-yard average.

On Saturday, they gained 139 yards on 39 runs. That 3.6-yard average might appear modest, but it stands up especially well considering that many of those runs came in the fourth quarter as they tried to run out the clock against the No. 3-ranked rushing defense in the NFL. It also helped that San Francisco lost All-Pro defensive tackle Bryant Young late in the first quarter to a neck injury that sidelined him the rest of the day.

Halfback Edgar Bennett did nothing but enhance his reputation as a mudder, gaining 80 yards and averaging 4.7 yards. He did that on a muddy field battered by a constant rain and a 20-mph wind that dropped the wind chill to 9 degrees.

"You get up here in December and January and watch our back run," Wolf said.

The Packers now have run for more than 100 yards in their last five games, four of which have been on slippery Lambeau.

That running game, as much as anything, has added to the Packers' air of invulnerability at home. They were able to control the ball on the ground without having to rely solely on Favre's playmaking.

Favre had a quiet but efficient day passing. He threw for only 79 yards — the last time he was limited to less than 100 yards was in 1994 — but he and his receivers handled the horrible throwing conditions much better than the 49ers. He completed 11-of-15 passes to seven different receivers, whereas San Francisco quarterbacks Steve Young and Elvis Grbac completed only 53 percent of their passes, with their receivers dropping at least five of those throws.

Next week's possible opponents are both warm-weather teams. So if the temperature turns colder by Sunday — the average in Green Bay on Jan. 12 is 22 degrees, and that's without factoring in the wind chill — so much the better from the Packers' perspective.

"Nobody feels invincible," receiver Antonio Freeman said. "(But) we're a football team on a mission. Invincible is a big word. We like our chances. I think that says it best."

Desmond Howard picks up speed on his 71-yard punt return for a touchdown in the first quarter against the Niners.

Packers Produce Instead of Panicking

BY CHRIS HAVEL
Press-Gazette

For all its muddy grandeur, there was a certain something missing Saturday as the Packers cruised to their 17th straight win at Lambeau Field.

Something beyond dry footing, any semblance of the 49ers' offense and Desmond Howard to start the second half.

That certain something, of course, was the Dallas Cowboys, who are doing their darndest to go from America's Team to America's Most Wanted (the TV show). Their presence was formally requested by 60,787 Saturday, who shouted, "We want Dallas! We want Dallas!" (not the TV show.)

The cry went up midway through the fourth quarter, approximately the same time the 49ers went down for the count in the 35-14 playoff loss. Packers GM Ron Wolf said he doesn't care who his team meets in the NFC championship game (wink, wink), but he understands the fans' yearning for the Cowboys.

"What better opportunity than to have a chance to get the monkey off your back in your own park with the team you've assembled to play in your park," he said. "It's what we've stressed all along. Now we have everything we've asked for. Now all we have to do is do it."

Translation: Carolina would make a delightful Super Bowl XXXI hors d'oevre, but no victory party would be complete without the Cowboys as the main course. And if somebody knocked the smirk off Michael Irvin's face, all the better.

The Packers likely will get the chance to do both soon enough.

Meantime, a rain-soaked romp over the 49ers will have to suffice.

Packers coach Mike Holmgren's most telling comment came before Saturday's game, not after it.

"We're trying to prove something," he said Thursday. "And they're trying to hold on to something."

What the Packers proved is they are the NFL's most dominant team. They made the once mighty 49ers look like a team that was wet behind the earholes.

The heck with pride. The 49ers had all they could do to hold onto the ball. They dropped six passes. They fumbled three times. They wallowed in the mud throughout the game. To their credit, they didn't wallow in self-pity after it.

San Francisco coach George Seifert correctly identified the difference between his team and Holmgren's.

It was the Packers' 12-play, 72-yard touchdown drive that came immediately after Howard was caught with his pants down. While the Packers' return ace was switching uniforms, his kick-return team was shorthanded. The result was a 49ers touchdown that pulled them to within 21-14.

The Packers didn't panic. They produced.

They ran 10 times for 50 yards and passed twice for 22. The clincher came when Edgar Bennett's goal-line fumble was retrieved by Antonio Freeman, who leapt from beneath the pile holding the football, and the victory, in his hand.

"That drive proved what a great team they really are," Seifert said. "That drive was the sign of a championship team."

It was reminiscent of the Cowboys' grinding touch-

Game 17 | JANUARY 4, 1997

It's lights out for the Niners at Lambeau Field as fans cheer the Packers. Next up: the NFC championship game.

down drive that sealed the Packers' fate in last year's NFC championship game. Except this time, Green Bay wasn't on the receiving end of the butt-kicking.

It wasn't Emmitt Smith, but Edgar Bennett doing the battering.

Bennett doesn't merely drive an all-terrain vehicle. He is an all-terrain vehicle. He ran for more yards (80) than Favre threw for (79). And Favre still had an MVP performance, completing 11 passes to seven targets.

The Packers' defense can be described in a word: Ouch.

Ditto for the special teams: Howard.

Make no mistake. The Panthers would be a worthy adversary, but it is the Cowboys who make the blood of Packers fans boil. It appears the Packers won't be denied. In a perfect world, neither will their fans.

New Sod For Lambeau

BY JOHN MORTON
Press-Gazette

GREEN BAY, JAN. 5, 1997 — Lambeau Field, reduced to mud after Saturday's rain-soaked game between the Packers and the 49ers, will be completely resodded before Sunday's NFC championship game, a league official said Sunday.

The sod will be cut today at a Maryland farm and loaded on tractor trailers for the journey to Green Bay, NFL spokesman Bill McConnell said. The resodding process will begin no later than Wednesday, he said.

The NFC championship game falls under the jurisdiction of the league. Chip Toma, the NFL's turf consultant, made the decision to resod the field, McConnell said. The Packers grounds crew will perform the labor, he said, but the NFL will pay for the sod.

The NFL also resodded the field for the 1995 NFC championship at San Francisco's Candlestick Park, now known at 3Com Park, McConnell said.

The Packers resodded the middle of Lambeau Field between the hashmarks before the Dec. 22 game between the Packers and Vikings.

After Saturday's game, a tarp was spread across the field to protect it, but significant damage had been done, Packers field supervisor Todd Edelback said.

That was after players had spent much of the game slipping and sliding, and shredding the turf.

The crews have a formidable task, said Ron Tillmann, the former owner of Tillmann Landscape Nursery in Green Bay.

First, what's left of the old sod must be removed. The ground below then must be flattened before the new sod is placed.

Tillmann said the new sod must be thick enough so it won't be torn apart easily by the players.

It won't have nearly enough time to take root. That usually takes a month to six weeks, he said.

Chuck Stevenson of Janesville was one of the many volunteers who helped work on the new field.

The new sod is rolled out at Lambeau Field before the NFC championship game.

Composed Packers quarterback Brett Favre shovels the ball to Dorsey Levens as he is tackled by a pair of Panthers.

Packers	0	17	10	3	30
Panthers	7	3	3	0	13

What A Rush!

By Pete Dougherty
Press-Gazette

GREEN BAY, JAN. 12, 1997 — The Green Bay Packers are running to New Orleans.

They certainly didn't appear to be a candidate for running their way to the top of NFL, considering they've spent the past five years building their identity around MVP quarterback Brett Favre's playmaking.

But in their ground game's most powerful statement to date, the Packers rushed for 201 yards in a decisive 30-13 victory over the Carolina Panthers in the NFC championship game Sunday at Lambeau Field.

It was the sixth straight game in which they've topped the 100-yard mark rushing. And most impressively, it came when they needed it most, with a trip to New Orleans for Super Bowl XXXI on the line, on a day when the wind chill hovered near minus-20, and against a defense that gave up the second-fewest points in the NFL this year.

"You look at the last four games, we've piled up big yards running the football," receiver Antonio Freeman said. "That's what championship teams are all about."

The 1-2 punch of Edgar Bennett and Dorsey Levens was the difference Sunday, and they combined for 187 of the 201 rushing yards. That helped neutralize

NFC Championship | PACKERS 30, PANTHERS 13

Ron Cox (left) and Brian Williams stuff the Panthers, limiting Carolina to only 45 yards rushing in the game.

the Panthers' 3-4 zone-blitzing scheme, which had produced an NFL-best 60 sacks and limited rattled opponents to an average of just 14 points in the regular season.

But Sunday, the Panthers sacked Favre only once and gave up the most points and total yards (479) they have all season.

"We just didn't have the opportunity to get into our pass rush because they ran the ball so well," said Lamar Lathon, a Pro Bowl linebacker for Carolina.

The Packers offense has come a long way from the seemingly one-dimensional unit that for the past four seasons couldn't run when Green Bay got deep into the playoffs. Sunday marked the second straight playoff game in which the Packers outrushed their opponents more than 2-1.

Last week in a divisional playoff game on a muddy, sloppy Lambeau Field, they pounded for 139 yards on the ground against a San Francisco 49ers defense that finished the regular season ranked No. 3 against the run.

In their last six games — four regular season, two playoff — the Packers averaged 152 yards rushing a game. Five of those six games have been at wintry Lambeau.

"Our biggest motivation was that all year, everyone has been saying our weakest point was our running game," Levens said. "We've been hearing that. We wanted to prove our point. We didn't ask anybody to give us respect. I guess we had to go out and take it."

Levens not only ran for 8.8 yards a carry, he also caught five passes for 117 yards, giving him one of the best playoff performances in Packers history. His 205 yards rushing and receiving set a team playoff record, breaking the 180 yards James Lofton gained against Dallas in January 1983.

Levens made three big plays that were especially crucial in turning an early struggle into a fourth-quar-

Dorsey Levens stiff-arms the Panthers en route to 88 yards rushing on only 10 attempts.

Brett Favre, who picked apart the Carolina defense for 292 yards passing, delivers a strike to Antonio Freeman.

ter celebration.

The first was when he busted a third-and-1 run for a 35-yard gain that set up the Packers' first touchdown.

The second was on the very next play, an athletic 29-yard reception in which he ran past and then jumped over one of the NFL's top cornerbacks, Eric Davis, for

"(The touchdown catch) was unusual because it was a running back against a (cornerback)," Freeman said. "But Dorsey's a fantastic athlete. He displayed that on the third-and-1 when he got through that first wave and opened it up."

Said receiver Don Beebe, "It shows you the depth we have. A guy like that can't even start on this team."

Though Carolina limited Dallas' Emmitt Smith to only 3.6 yards a carry last week, the Packers' film studies convinced them they could run on the Panthers, if not consistently, then at least for a big hit every now and then. Carolina's 3-4 blitzing and stunting scheme generally doesn't rush more than four or five players, but it tries to overload one side of the line or the other. Their goal is to flood a gap with more blitzers than there are men to block them.

Helped by an offensive line that controlled the line much of the day, Bennett and Levens found enough gaps to average a robust 5.3 yards a carry and pop eight runs of 7 yards or more. Bennett rushed for a game-high 99 yards on 25 carries.

"Sometimes they blitzed themselves right out of the hole," Packers center Frank Winters said of Carolina.

The Packers' dominating run helped take the pressure off Favre, who struggled early in the game.

He completed only three of his first nine passes and threw an interception deep in Packers territory that set up Carolina for 7-0 lead in the first quarter. The last time the Packers trailed in a game was Dec. 1, when Chicago jumped to a 7-0 lead.

"There's been times when (the offensive line) has messed up and Brett's helped us out," Winters said. "It was our turn."

Favre went on to complete 16 of his final 20 passes, giving him a 19-for-29 game for 292 yards. It marked the fifth straight game in which the Packers have scored at least 30 points and should help make them a strong favorite to beat New England in the Super Bowl on Jan. 26.

the catch in the end zone. And the third was a 66-yard screen pass in the third quarter that beat a Carolina blitz and set up the touchdown that gave the Packers a 27-13 lead.

Players Happy To Share Title With Fans

By Chris Havel

Press-Gazette

When the euphoria in Titletown finally wanes, if it wanes, the lasting image from Sunday's NFC championship game will be that of a team and a town who truly deserve one another.

It is difficult to know which is grittier. The Packers, who twice erased early deficits to destroy the capable Carolina Panthers, 30-13. Or a rugged Lambeau Field crowd of 60,216 that stayed to the frigid, beautiful end.

The payoff was the franchise's first trip to the Super Bowl since 1968.

To the Packers' diehard fans, the minus–17 wind chill was as irrelevant as the Panthers' zone blitz. They came dressed for success, not to be denied by something as incidental as the elements.

"This is an unbelievable setting," said Packers general manager Ron Wolf, a man not prone to exaggeration. "If this doesn't move an individual, nothing will. To witness all that happened, particularly after the game. ... The crowd stayed and the crowd cheered and the crowd has always given us magnificent support."

Reggie White summed it up in his postgame speech, "Green Bay, I hope you're proud of us, because we're proud of you."

The crowd shouted its reply: "Regg-EE! Regg-EE!"

There is nothing to match the bond that is formed

Wayne Simmons and friends have a lot to shout about — the Packers are headed to the Super Bowl.

throughout years of heartache and an afternoon of ecstasy. The frozen tundra? More like a warm fuzzy. This was the feel-good show of the year. Virginia McCaskey, the daughter of Chicago Bears founder George S. Halas, added a dose of dignity to the postgame proceedings when she presented the trophy that bears her father's name.

"Congratulations," she said, her voice rising above the crowd, "to Bob Harlan, Ron Wolf, Coach Holmgren, the players and your fans ... "

Coming from a lifelong Bears fan, it was a supreme compliment.

It triggered a resounding cheer.

And the Packers' fans had plenty to cheer about this day.

There was the Packers' running game. Talk about four-wheelin' with feelin'. Edgar Bennett and Dorsey Levens are an all-terrain terror.

They are The Thing With Four Legs, a relentless monstrosity that eats up ground and opposing defenses alike. They combined for 187 yards on 35 carries. That's 5.3 yards per ramble.

There was Brett Favre.

The NFL's two-time Most Valuable Player extended his home record to 19-0 in cold weather home games. He is part Mississippian, part polar bear. He hit on 19-of-29 passes for 292 yards and two touchdowns.

Favre's most amazing play came early in the second half, when he scrambled away from one Panthers linebacker and into Kevin Greene's arms. Rather than panic, the master of ingenuity threw a chest pass to Levens for a first down.

Said Favre, "Kevin got up and just goes, 'Wow!' "

Greene wasn't the only one.

The Packers' defense was no less impressive. It limited the Panthers to a pair of field goals and a 2-yard touchdown drive. Rookie cornerback Tyrone Williams played like a veteran and 12-year pro Eugene Robinson ran around like a rookie.

Defensive coordinator Fritz Shurmur's troops stuffed the Panthers' running game with seven-man fronts, one fewer defender than most teams failed with.

After the game, there were a fair number of tears shed in the locker room.

Packers president Bob Harlan, never one to make a scene, couldn't avoid it. He got choked up in mid-interview. After 26 frustrating years with the Packers, he was allowed to let go of his emotions.

"I was a wreck all week," he admitted. "This was the most impactful game I've ever been associated with."

Twenty feet away, cornerback Doug Evans brushed back a tear. Way back in August, he dedicated this season to his father, who had passed away.

"I felt like he was watching over me and good things were going to happen to this team," he said. "I could really feel that."

No one doubted the Louisiana native, who added, "Mom, I'm going home."

Across the way, receiver Don Beebe was reveling in his fifth trip to the Super Bowl in eight seasons.

"I'm spoiled," he admitted.

For one glorious season, at least, so is one town and its team.

Super Bowl I | JANUARY 15, 1967

Packers	7	7	14	7	35
Chiefs	0	10	0	0	10

Defending NFL's Honor

BY CHRIS HAVEL
Press-Gazette

GREEN BAY — The legend of Super Bowl I has grown through the years. Bart Starr's calm efficiency, Vince Lombardi's inspirational halftime speech and Max McGee's late-night escapades have become a part of football's folklore that will live forever.

It has been 30 years since the Green Bay Packers defended the National Football League's honor in a 35-10 victory over the American Football League's Kansas City Chiefs. To the colorful cast that played in that game on Jan. 15, 1967, it doesn't seem nearly so long. Those players know that what they achieved that day carries historical significance that spans the decades.

The Packers' most vivid recollection of that first "World Championship" played at the Los Angeles Coliseum has to do with the pressure they felt. Willie Davis, the Packers' powerful defensive left end, described it as very real and very intense.

"The main difference between then and

**Left: Bart Starr, MVP of Super Bowl I, is swarmed under by the Chiefs.
Right: Vince Lombardi's goal was to embarrass the AFL in the first Super Bowl.**

now is it was happening for the first time," Davis said. "Here you had new guys challenging the old establishment. We were not just carrying the banner of NFL versus AFL. We also carried the banner of expectations that we were supposed to win. That placed us in a very tough position. It went from that to, 'How big should you win?'

"We had a job to do and my attitude was, 'What better team to do it than the Packers?' "

On that sunny California day, the Coliseum drew a crowd of 63,036, with a record TV audience of more than 70 million watching around the nation. Those are modest numbers by comparison to the Super Bowls that have followed. Initially, pro football fans were cool on the game. Even Lombardi had a difficult time mustering much enthusiasm.

It wasn't until NFL commissioner Pete Rozelle telephoned

Super Bowl I | PACKERS 35, CHIEFS 10

Lombardi at the team's Santa Barbara headquarters that the legendary coach decide to promote Super Bowl I.

"Lombardi didn't really even like the name 'Super Bowl' at first," noted Los Angeles Times sports columnist Jim Murray. "It was the invention of (Chiefs owner) Lamar Hunt. It took Lombardi a long time to warm up to the idea of the game."

Lombardi believed his Packers already had won *the* "World Championship" with their 34-27 victory over the Dallas Cowboys on New Year's Day. Why play a game, Lombardi thought, if there was nothing to gain and everything to lose.

"It might not have been a big game for the public, or the fans, but it was for us," said Fuzzy Thurston, the Packers' left guard. "Here we had the weight of the whole league on us to beat this brand-new team. I know Vince felt like he was carrying the weight of the league on his shoulders."

The realization that the game would be played despite Lombardi's objections altered the attitude of the Hall of Fame coach. By golly, he thought, if we have to play this game, let's embarrass the AFL's representative. Maybe then they'll think twice about wanting to step onto the field with an NFL team.

Lombardi's attitude quickly filtered down to his players. Jerry Kramer, the team's right guard, sensed the urgency in his head coach.

"First of all, we'd already won the championship," Kramer said. "The AFL was not highly regarded by the NFL. So we wanted to belittle them as much as we could. Coach Lombardi had the pressure on him to beat them. And beat them badly."

The tone was set.

It was the upstart Chiefs versus the proud and mighty Packers.

Green Bay had endured just two losses by a total of four points that season. They fell to the San Fran-

cisco 49ers, 21-20, in early October and were upset by the Minnesota Vikings, 20-17, a month later. After that, they ground out seven straight victories en route to Super Bowl I.

The Packers' roster was replete with future Hall of Famers.

The offense featured Starr at quarterback, Forrest Gregg at right tackle and Jim Taylor at fullback. All are represented by busts in Canton, Ohio. They were buoyed by receiver Carroll Dale, running back Elijah Pitts and tight end Marv Fleming.

Starr, a 17th-round draft pick in 1956, led the NFL in passing that season. The four-time Pro Bowler was noted for his cool demeanor and savvy ways. He also had a toughness that belied his boyish looks.

Taylor was playing what turned out to be his final season with the Packers. The bruising fullback wanted to go out a champion.

Gregg, of course, was a machine on the right side. He went to eight straight Pro Bowls and would be voted on the NFL's 75th anniversary all-time team.

Defensively, the Packers were even more talented. This unit featured an amazing five future Hall of Famers in the starting lineup. There was middle linebacker Ray Nitschke, whose balding head and missing front teeth, not to mention his lateral speed and crushing tackles, were enough to strike fear into any opposing quarterback. There was Herb Adderley, the swift All-Pro cornerback who lived up to his status as a first-round draft choice out of Michigan State.

There was Davis, the pass-rushing end who blossomed after coming to the Packers in a 1960 trade with the Cleveland Browns. Powerful tackle Henry Jordan manned the interior line like a junkyard dog, relentlessly pursuing any ballcarrier who dared to come near.

Backing them up was free safety Willie Wood, a free agent whose nose for the ball led him to 48 career interceptions. He is one of only six free agents to be

Paul Hornung (5), who was unable to play in Super Bowl I because of an injury, and Jerry Kramer (64) led the Packers to many memorable wins in the 1960's.

inducted into the Hall of Fame.

"We had a great deal of confidence in ourselves and our ability," said Bob Skoronski, the starting left tackle. "We just refused to accept the fact that somebody could beat us."

But the Chiefs did not lack talent.

Kansas City's explosive offense featured Len Dawson at quarterback, Otis Taylor at wide receiver and Mike Garrett at halfback. The left side of the offensive line was anchored by stalwarts Jim Tyrer at tackle and Ed Budde at guard.

Defensively, right tackle Buck Buchanon paved the way for a unit that included Jerry Mays at left end, Bobby Bell at left outside linebacker and E.J. Holub at right linebacker.

The Chiefs did not lack pride, either.

Left cornerback Fred (The Hammer) Williamson

predicted he would knock out the Packers' ballcarriers with his devastating tackles. And Buchanon was as fine a tackle to ever play the game.

The Chiefs didn't feel like they had to back down to anybody. Not even the powerful Packers.

Still, the Packers were unimpressed. Kramer remembers strong safety Bobby Hunt and right corner Willie Mitchell getting tangled up in the Chiefs' defensive backfield early in the game.

"It could've happened to anybody," Kramer said. "And McGee says, 'Welcome to Looney Tunes and Merry Melodies.' The guy I was going up against (Andy Rice) wasn't that great, so I didn't notice Bell, Buchanon and those guys. I didn't see what great players they really were."

It took just two quarters for the Packers to change their minds. The Chiefs were indeed a formidable

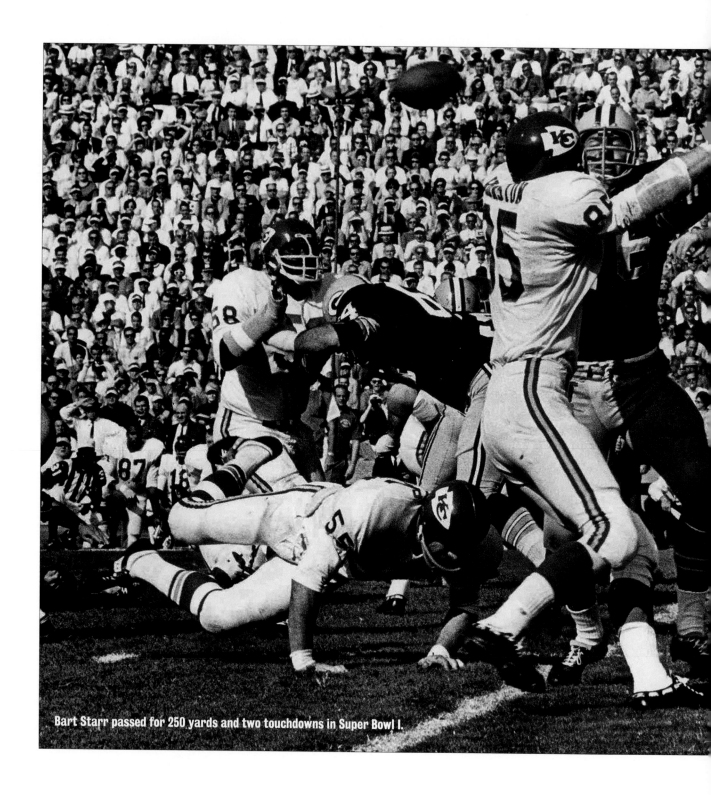

Bart Starr passed for 250 yards and two touchdowns in Super Bowl I.

opponent. They weren't going to allow them to win, but at least they were convinced the Chiefs deserved to be on the same field.

"Kansas City, talent-wise, later proved they were capable of beating anybody," Davis said. "All they lacked was experience and savvy. If we hadn't employed all of our experience and knowledge of how to win, it could have been an embarrassing afternoon for us."

The Packers won the opening coin toss and elected to receive.

They took over at their own 25-yard line and netted a first down as adversity struck. Receiver Boyd Dowler went down with an injury and was replaced by McGee. The 34-year-old veteran allegedly had been out partying the previous night. He had played sparingly throughout the season and had no idea he'd be called upon to play a prominent role.

McGee recalled telling roommate Paul Hornung the day before the game, "If something happens to Boyd, I'm not sure I'd be able to go the route. I haven't played too much this year, you know."

Nevertheless, McGee trotted onto the field and into the huddle. He wasted little time in making an impact. After the teams traded possessions, he made a one-handed catch at the Kansas City 23-yard line that resulted in a 37-yard touchdown. It remains one of the most famous plays in Super Bowl history.

Thurston called McGee's performance the surprise of the day.

"He came off the bench and caught those passes like he never caught them before," Thurston said. "I'm not sure why. I guess it's because he hadn't been to bed. That's the story anyway. He's never actually admitted to anyone what happened."

McGee said he had a good game because he was not expecting to play and therefore was loose, without pregame jitters.

Against the Chiefs McGee finished with seven

Super Bowl I | PACKERS 35, CHIEFS 10

catches for 138 yards and two touchdowns. McGee said he might've scored on a 37-yard pass from Starr late in the fourth quarter if he had been in better shape.

"I was kind of trying to find a place to fall down," he admitted.

Al Silverman, then the editor at *Sport* magazine, said McGee nearly edged out Starr for MVP honors. But the voters decided to go with Starr on the merit of his "excellent overall play."

Starr completed 16-of-23 passes for 250 yards and two TD's and one interception. Lombardi said the success stemmed from the Chiefs' decision to play an eight-man front.

The Packers rushed 34 times for 133 yards, but had trouble early in the game moving the ball on the ground.

After the game, Lombardi said, "There is no way you can run against stacked defenses. Or, I should say, you can run against 'em, but it's not easy. It is easy to pass against, however. They were daring us to throw."

The Chiefs, of course, didn't go down without a fight. Dawson moved them 66 yards in six plays early in the second quarter to even the score at 7-7. He hit running back Curtis McClinton on a 7-yard touchdown pass with 10:40 to play in the half.

The Packers responded with a 13-play, 73-yard TD drive, capped by Taylor's 14-yard run around left end to make it 14-7.

Undaunted, the Chiefs answered by moving 50 yards as the first half winded down. Mike Mercer drilled a 31-yard field goal with 54 seconds remaining to slice the Packers' lead to a rather precarious 14-10.

Enter Lombardi.

The legendary coach with the gap-tooth grin wasn't smiling.

He told his team to "stop grabbing and start tackling." Davis recalls the halftime speech vividly.

"Before the game, Lombardi said we had to go out and play and not make a big mistake to allow the Chiefs to take advantage," Davis said. "We played the first 30 minutes adhering to that. Then at halftime, Lombardi said, 'Look, we've played 30 minutes of football adjusting to the Chiefs, to make sure nothing bad happened. All I ask now is you play 30 minutes of Packers football and see how the Chiefs adjust to you.' "

Davis said the team was inspired.

"We walked out a different team," he said. "We played with the abandon and like the reckless team on defense that we were."

Kramer concurred.

"The game was over at halftime," Kramer said. "They were a little awed by the Green Bay legend. They felt happy they didn't embarrass themselves in the first half. After Pitts scored early in the second half, we were lining up for the extra point and the kid against me, he just leaned on me with all the force of a feather duster. That hadn't ever happened to me before. Right then I knew the game was over."

The Packers went on to score three second-half touchdowns while shutting out the Chiefs.

Green Bay's vaunted defense sacked Dawson six times and limited the speedy Garrett to just 17 yards on six carries. The Chiefs lost much of their fight when Williamson, who'd predicted he'd use "The Hammer" on the Packers, was knocked out when Donny Anderson's knee caught him square on the chin.

After the game, the Packers gave Lombardi the game ball. It was the third time he'd been so honored. One writer wanted to know if the ball Lombardi received was an NFL or AFL ball.

"An NFL ball," said Lombardi. "It catches a little bit better and it kicks a little bit better than the AFL ball."

Now, of course, the pressure was off. Lombardi's Packers had successfully defended the NFL's honor. But a new era was dawning in professional football.

Super Bowl I | JANUARY 15, 1967

The Chiefs had won, too, because they had proven AFL teams could compete.

The difference on that sunny California day, according to Davis, was experience.

"We knew how to win," he said. "We knew how better to control those factors — momentum, the unusual early excitement, how to work our way through trouble and not panic. Those were the reasons we beat the Chiefs. When everything was on the line we came through and convinced the world that if you're going to get to the top of the heap in the NFL, you had to come through the Green Bay Packers."

Beginning in 1961, the Packers won five NFL championships and two Super Bowls in seven seasons.

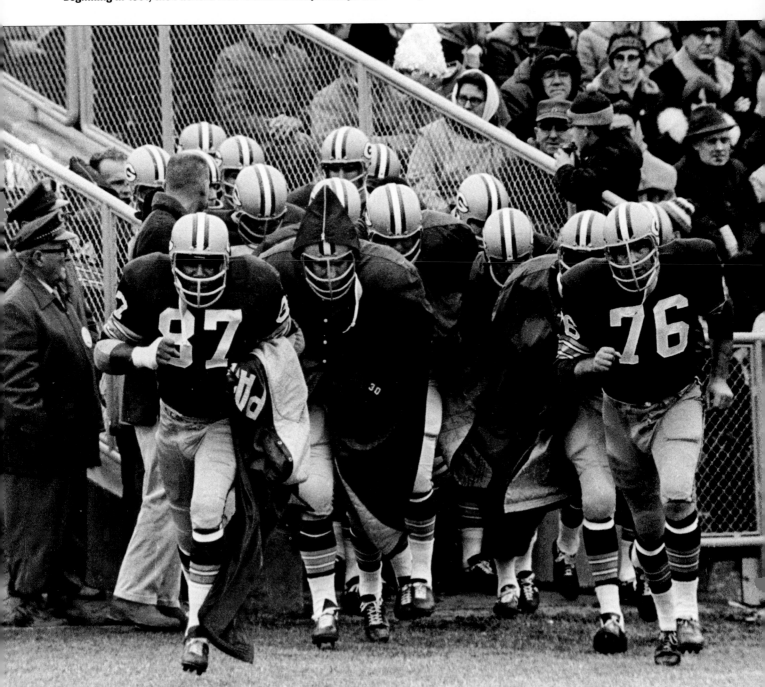

Championship Journal

By Mike Holmgren
As told to Chris Havel and John U. Bacon

MONDAY, JAN. 13, 1997 — It's Day One after the NFC championship win over Carolina and the Super Bowl frenzy has just started.

MONDAY, JAN. 13

7:30 A.M. — *Radio interview with Wisconsin stations. After an exciting NFC championship, our Wisconsin media are excited about hearing our Super Bowl plans.*

9 A.M. — *Tape two editions of the Mike Holmgren Show at WBAY. One will air tonight, the other next Monday.*

11 A.M. — *Meet with team to discuss Super Bowl plans and schedule for upcoming week. We want to keep things as normal as possible to keep our players focused on the task at hand.*

NOON — *Meet with the NFL to discuss media requests and scheduling for Super Bowl week in New Orleans.*

Today I spent one hour giving interviews with Wisconsin radio stations, taped two editions of the Mike Holmgren Show, then met with NFL personnel to handle media requests for Super Bowl week. I also met with my secretary to discuss logistical preparations, and with our team to keep our heads straight the next two weeks.

Over the next two weeks, I'll give dozens of interviews and sign thousands of autographs. But this is what it's all about. This is what we've been building for these past five years.

TUESDAY, JAN. 14, 1997 — At 12:30 I picked up my daughter, Emily, at home and took her to see my mother, Barbara Holmgren, at the nursing home before Emily headed back to Gordon College in Boston, where she's a sophomore.

My mom cried a little when she talked about this season and the Super Bowl — much like mothers do. Unfortunately, she can't be in New Orleans because of her illness, rheumatoid arthritis and diabetes. She's confined to a wheelchair, which isn't much fun. But this excitement helps her. She's going to watch it on TV and root just as hard.

My wife, Kathy, gets a little nervous about these games. We're bringing family in from California, Minnesota and Boston, so this is really going to be a family event. They're all going to have a great time down there, and Kathy will worry for everyone.

Today is also a real treat because I'll get to watch my daughter Gretchen's junior varsity basketball game. I don't get to see Gretchen play a whole lot, but when I do, I try to sneak in as best I can, which is hard to do at some of these gyms. Gretchen's at that age where things I do embarrass her, so I just try to stay quiet and watch the game.

For the most part, people let me watch her play. I've only had one guy come up to me and start talking about what I thought about her coach's strategy. I'm thinking, "Hey I'm just here to watch my daughter play. I have enough worries with that other game — football."

CHAMPIONSHIP JOURNAL

Mike Holmgren savored the win over Carolina and then turned his sights on the Super Bowl.

I've only given Gretchen two pieces of advice. One, quit messing with your hair while you're playing. Just put it up there and leave it. Often, when you watch girls play basketball, they're always fiddling with their hair. Two, quit messing with your jersey. You look fine. Just play.

Gretchen works really hard out there.

12:30 P.M. — *Press conference.*

4 P.M. — *Meet with PR staff to discuss media policies and interview requests for myself and for the team.*

4:30 P.M. — *Workout on the treadmill.*

5:30 P.M. — *Game plan for Super Bowl.*

TUESDAY, JAN. 14

12:30 P.M. — *Pick up my daughter Emily at home and take her to see my mother at the nursing home before Emily heads back to Boston, where she is a sophomore at Gordon College.*

1:30 P.M. — *Take Emily to the airport.*

2:30 P.M. — *Interview with Dick Schaap for a Packers book he is writing.*

4 P.M — *Workout on the treadmill.*

5 P.M. — *Meet with coaches to work on game plan.*

WEDNESDAY, JAN. 15

9 A.M. — *Team and position meetings begin for the week.*

9:30 A.M. — *Interview with Peter King of Sports Illustrated for Super Bowl preview issue.*

11:15 A.M. — *Team practice.*

11:45 A.M. — *Press conference.*

Mike Holmgren's Diary

12:15 P.M. — *Interview with Alan Shipnuck of Sports Illustrated.*

1 P.M. — *On-camera interview with Ed Werder of CNN/Sports Illustrated.*

1:30 P.M. — *The first of our full practices in preparation for Super Bowl.*

3 P.M. — *Haircut.*

4:30 P.M. — *Photo shoot with Brett Favre at Kroll's Restaurant for Sports Illustrated Super Bowl preview issue.*

THURSDAY, JAN. 16

7:15 A.M. — *Radio interviews.*

9 A.M. — *Team and position meetings.*

11:15 A.M. — *Team practice.*

1:30 p.m. — *Team practice. We are slowing implementing the game plan. The extra week gives us the opportunity to fine tune things.*

4 P.M. — *Workout on the treadmill.*

FRIDAY, JAN. 17

9 A.M. — *Team and position meetings.*

11:45 A.M. — *Final full practice of the week. The players appear to be focused as we prepare to depart for New Orleans.*

12:45 P.M. — *Press conference.*

1 P.M. — *On-camera interview with Fox TV.*

I love watching her run up and down the court. It's one of the true joys in life to watch her play. When she's on the court, no one thinks about who her dad is. Gretchen has a lot of friends, and they're her friends because she's Gretchen, not because she's Mike Holmgren's daughter.

WEDNESDAY, JAN. 15, 1997 — Since the players had yesterday off, the coaches sat down to start work on our game plan. No head coach gets to the Super Bowl without top-shelf coaches, and I've got 'em.

The meetings were intense but productive. Sherm Lewis, our offensive coordinator, is working like crazy this time of year, but I can tell when something is bothering him. Since we're still playing other teams can't talk to him, but he sees all these head coaching jobs opening up and other guys getting them while we're getting ready for the Super Bowl.

He wants to be a head coach and he should be a head coach, and these other guys are getting these jobs. I remember having the same feeling.

The fact that he's the offensive coordinator here doesn't help him as much as it should. Sherm Lewis is one of the best offensive coordinators in the game, but he doesn't get the credit he deserves because people say he's the offensive coordinator for an offensive coach, so they figure he doesn't do that much. Nothing could be further from the truth. I've tried to explain this many times, but it doesn't seem to stick.

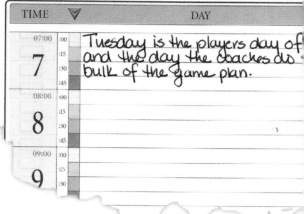

Tuesday is the players day off and the day the coaches do bulk of the game plan.

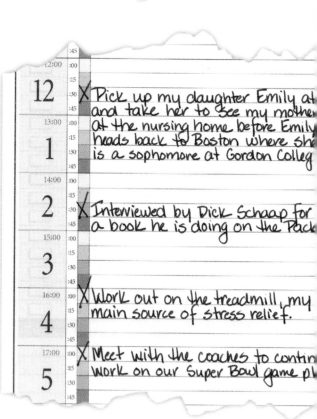

12:30 X Pick up my daughter Emily at and take her to see my mother at the nursing home before Emily heads back to Boston where she is a sophomore at Gordon College

2:30 X Interviewed by Dick Schaap for a book he is doing on the Pack

4:00 X Work out on the treadmill, my main source of stress relief.

5:00 X Meet with the coaches to contin work on our Super Bowl game pl

I told him, if he thought it would allow him to reach his dream sooner, he could take another job for a more defensive-minded head coach, but he said, "No, I love it here."

Still, I know it hurts him. That's why I will do everything I possibly can to help him get a head coaching job.

THURSDAY, JAN. 16, 1997 — Another day of practice for the team. We are slowly implementing the game plan for the Super Bowl. The extra week gives us the opportunity to fine tune things as we go along. Of course, we have to remember the Patriots have the same opportunity, and Bill Parcells is not likely to waste it, either.

FRIDAY, JAN. 17, 1997 — We had our final, full practice of the week this morning. The players seem to be keeping their focus as we get ready to leave for New Orleans — a good sign.

It's been an incredibly busy week — a week like no other — but we've accomplished what we set out to do so far. We've put together the bulk of our game plan, and we've had real good practices. We'll put in the remainder of our plans next week.

I've tried to educate the players as to what they can expect to see in New Orleans, and what we expect from them, because Super Bowl week is like nothing you're ever been through. Don Beebe, Jim McMahon and Sherm Lewis have all been there, so they talked to the guys about the experience. Everyone was listening. They want to do it right.

Still, there is a difference between practicing like you're playing this Sunday and practicing like you're playing next week — which, of course, we are. The sense of urgency wasn't there like it normally would be, but that's OK. The mental part, the groundwork for the Super Bowl has been established.

SATURDAY, JAN. 18, 1997 — I met with the team for the final time until we reach New Orleans. I have a feeling next week is going to be a good one.

SUNDAY, JAN. 19, 1997 — Upon our arrival at the New Orleans airport this afternoon, more than 300 Packer fans greeted us with their loud support. There are no other groups like them in the NFL.

Later, when we checked into the Fairmont Hotel — well, the realization struck. In Green Bay, we were planning and practicing and working hard, but in the back of my mind I knew and everyone else knew we had another week. Well, this is New Orleans — and this is it.

We've had a good season, and things have fallen into place nicely. No doubt, the organization is more prepared to handle all the pressures and frenzy of a Super Bowl than we would have been last year. But no matter how prepared you are, it's still Star Wars once you finally get down here. That's why we had a team meeting tonight to establish the ground rules, poli-

SATURDAY, JAN. 18
9 A.M. — *Final team and position meetings until we reach New Orleans.*
9:30 A.M. — *Interview with former Packers receiver James Lofton.*
9:45 A.M. — *Interview with Chris Havel of the Green Bay Press-Gazette.*
10:30 A.M. — *Light team practice.*

SUNDAY, JAN. 19
11 A.M. — *Drop off luggage in the gym at the stadium.*
12:15 P.M. — *Buses depart for Austin Straubel Airport.*
1 P.M. — *Flight leaves for New Orleans.*
3:30 P.M. — *Arrive in New Orleans to a very enthusiastic crowd of Packer fans. More than 300 people greet us at the airport.*
4:15 P.M. — *Buses arrive at Fairmont Hotel. The team is met by a large group of reporters and photographers.*
5 P.M. — *Press conference.*
7:45 P.M. — *Team meeting to establish ground rules, policies and procedures for the week.*
8:30 P.M. — *Team snack.*

MONDAY, JAN. 20
8:15 A.M. — *Radio*

THE ROAD TO SUPER BOWL XXXI | **141**

Mike Holmgren's Diary

interviews with Wisconsin media.

9:30 A.M. — *Team breakfast.*

10:30 A.M. — *Team and position meetings at hotel. We continue to fine tune our game plan.*

NOON — *Team lunch.*

2 P.M. — *First practice at New Orleans Saints facility.*

5 P.M. — *Press conference for myself and selected players in ballroom at Fairmont Hotel.*

6 P.M. — *Workout on the treadmill in my room.*

7:30 P.M. — *Dinner at Ruth's Chris Restaurant.*

TUESDAY, JAN. 21

7:30 A.M. — *Team breakfast.*

8 A.M. — *Depart for media day at the Superdome.*

8:30 A.M. — *Press conference at the Superdome. I am honored as the VISA Coach of the Year. Fans vote on this award, which means a great deal to me. A check for $10,000 is presented to Freedom House in Green Bay on my behalf.*

8:45 A.M. — *Media day. I have never seen so many flash bulbs and microphones in my life. Our players are very cordial and patient with the media.*

11 A.M. — *Team and position meetings at*

cies and procedures for the week.

This is that time when personalities change. People start yelling at each other. It can get real crazy. You don't know about it until you've been through it once.

When Sherm and I were down in New Orleans before with the 49ers, we were just position coaches. We didn't have to call the game, so we had a chance to hang out some at a jazz club down there. Then when I became a coordinator, there was no time for that. And now, with all the responsibility of being a head coach, all that is obviously out of the question. I'll try to enjoy it as much as possible, but I'll feel like I'm cheating someone if I don't work as hard as possible during this week.

MONDAY, JAN. 20, 1997 — We finally had our first practice in New Orleans, and the players were clearly very excited. Me, too. For all the stuff that you have to do that goes into this game — press conferences, interviews, trying to touch base with friends in town for the game — where I'm most comfortable is on the practice field, doing my thing.

We're back to the real work of practice. Not a day too soon.

TUESDAY, JAN. 21, 1997 — I was honored to be selected as the VISA

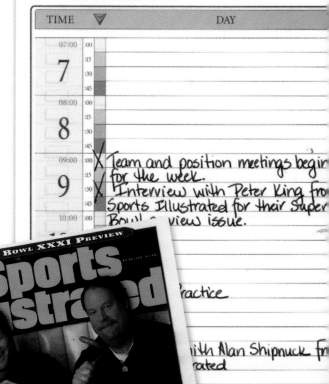

Holmgren and his prize pupil, Brett Favre, at the Saints practice field.

Coach of the Year. Fans vote on his award, which means a great deal to me. VISA also donates a check for $10,000 to the Freedom House in Green Bay on my behalf.

I've gotten a lot of congratulatory notes and phone calls. When we went out to dinner last night a couple guys, coaching friends, stopped by at our table to express their congratulations, which I appreciated. I think there's a sincerity there, which I appreciate. They know how hard it to get to this game, and now it's finally here.

Having the respect of my peers is important to me, and I think perhaps getting here shows people you can coach in this league. But I don't want a Super Bowl

the hotel.

NOON — Team lunch.

2 P.M. — Team practice at Saints facility.

4 P.M. — Workout on the treadmill.

WEDNESDAY, JAN. 22

8 A.M. — Team breakfast.

8:30 A.M. — "Mini media day" at the hotel, which includes a press conference for myself and media access to the entire team in one of the ballrooms. More flash bulbs and microphones.

9:45 A.M. — Meet with my administrative assistant, Sue Kluck, to make sure I am on track with my schedule for the week, and to make sure preparations have been made for my family arriving tomorrow morning.

10:30 A.M. — Team meeting.

10:45 A.M. — Review film in my office at the hotel. They have a beautiful office set up for myself, Ron Wolf and our staff. They have been taking excellent care of us throughout the week.

NOON — Team lunch.

2 P.M. — Practice at Saints facility. I want to take advantage of the warm weather with a motorcycle ride after practice, but I get caught in the rain and get soaked.

Mike Holmgren's Diary

4:30 P.M. — *Work-out on the treadmill.*

THURSDAY,
JAN. 23

8 A.M. — *Team breakfast.*

8:30 A.M. — *Another round of interviews for the players and coaches.*

10:30 A.M. — *Team and position meetings.*

2 P.M. — *Practice at the Saints facility. The players are very focused and have been practicing well. It is hard to block out all the distractions, but I think our guys are doing a good job.*

4 P.M. — *All of our families arrive this afternoon on the charter from Green Bay. Kathy and the girls are excited about being here, as are my son-in-laws.*

8 P.M. — *Dinner with my family at Commander's Palace.*

FRIDAY,
JAN. 24

8 A.M. — *Team breakfast.*

8:30 A.M. — *Press conference at the Hyatt Regency. This is my last press conference before the Super Bowl.*

11:45 A.M. — *Practice at the Saints facility. Heavy rain cause us to cancel practice after 10 minutes. The field is too slippery and I don't want our guys to get hurt. I attempt another motorcycle ride, but once again, I*

to change me or my life, my approach to my work or my family or anything else. I don't think it will change me all that much.

Still, when we had our first media day at the Superdome this morning, I've never seen so many flash bulbs and microphones in my life. I was proud of our players, who were very cordial and patient in the face of the deluge of questions they received.

Despite all the rigors and work, being in a Super Bowl is simply a great experience, and I'm really happy for my players. I've been to a couple of these and it's really fun. They're going to love it.

WEDNESDAY, JAN. 22, 1997 — My office at the Fairmont Hotel is like my home away from home. They're taking great care of us here.

THURSDAY, JAN. 23, 1997 — One break I do allow myself is spending as much time with my family as the schedule allows. My peaceful domain was invaded by all the women in my life this afternoon when they arrived.

I'm always concerned when they're all on one plane coming down until I see them again. It's valuable cargo on that plane.

Once we all got together again, we had a few laughs and they talked like they always do — all at once. We went out for a birthday dinner for Emily at Commander's Palace. What a terrific restaurant. We had a lovely dinner and a great time. That was really nice. So nice, I actually stopped thinking about the game for a little while.

22 **1997 JANUARY**
WEDNESDAY

TIME	DAY
07:00	
7	
08:00	✗ Team Breakfast
8	✗ Mini Media Day at the Fairmont. Inc a press conference for myself and media access to the entire team in one of the ballrooms. More flash bu and microphones.
09:00	
9	
10:00	✗ Meet with my administrative assistant Sue Kluck to make sure I am on track with my schedule for the week and to make sure that all the preparations have been made for my family arriving tomorrow afternoon.
10	
11:00	✗ Team Meeting
11	✗ Review film in my "temporary" office
12:00	✗ Team Lunch
12	
13:00	
1	
14:00	✗ Practice at the New Orleans Saints Facility. I thought I would take advantage of the warm weather by taking a motorcycle ride after practice, but I got caught in the rain and got soaked.
2	
15:00	
3	
16:00	
4	✗ Work out on the treadmill

Holmgren brought the Packers' third Lombardi Trophy back to Titletown.

The only trouble is, the girls are so involved in the football game, they're just as curious as everybody else and couldn't stop asking questions. Finally, I had to call a truce, put an end to the Holmgren Family Press Conference and get back to enjoying a great evening away from the game.

FRIDAY, JAN. 24, 1997 — Practice is cut short today because of rain. I don't want anyone getting hurt.

SATURDAY, JAN. 25, 1997 — We're practicing in the Superdome today, the last one before the tomorrow's game. The players will be on their normal Saturday schedule. They know all the preparation, all the hard work they've done for seven months — it's all right there, in this last practice. There's a certain finality to it.

SUNDAY, JAN. 26, 1997 — We treat today the same way we'd approach a normal Sunday night game. You have to kick everything up a couple hours. We let them sleep in a little bit — those who could — then had breakfast and started our meetings at noon. They had a little time off for those who wanted to go to mass or chapel services.

Then, four hours before the Super Bowl kickoff, we had our pre-game meal — the last supper, if you will.

Then the buses arrived to take us over to the Superdome. Once I got on this bus, I was pretty deep in thought, as usual. I'm looking at my sideline sheet, a little more than normal, but now we're ready to play the game.

The butterflies have already started. Once kick off arrives, everything will be all right.

... The game is over and we're Super Bowl champions. I'm too tired to write too much, but it's a great feeling. All the hard work has paid off.

get soaked. I think I'll wait until spring to try this again.

1:15 P.M. — Interview with Chris Havel.

SATURDAY, JAN. 25

7:30 A.M. — Team breakfast.

8:30 A.M. — Team and position meetings.

10 A.M. — Practice at the Superdome. As we get closer to the game you can feel the excitement increasing. We just have a light walkthrough. This is the last time we will practice before the game. The players appear loose and ready.

11:15 A.M. — Interview with Andrea Kremer of ESPN.

7 P.M. — Early dinner with my family at the Sazerac restaurant.

9 P.M. — Team meeting. I emphasize to the team this is the most important game we will ever play.

SUNDAY, JAN. 26

9:30 A.M. — Team breakfast.

10:30 A.M. — Team and position meetings. This is the last chance to fine tune the game plan and emphasize our strategy.

12:15 P.M. — Pregame chapel.

1:15 P.M. — Pregame meal.

5:21 P.M. — Kickoff.

Packers	10	17	8	0	35
Patriots	14	0	7	0	21

Super Bowl Champs

By Pete Dougherty
Press-Gazette

New Orleans, Jan. 26, 1997 — From start to finish this year, the Green Bay Packers simply packed the biggest punch in the NFL.

They showed it early in 1996, and they showed when it mattered most: During their stretch run to the NFL championship.

The title became official Sunday, when they returned the Vince Lombardi Trophy to its namesake's home after a 29-year wait with their 35-21 win over the game New England Patriots in Super Bowl XXXI at the Superdome.

The win culminated a five-year climb for the Packers, who as recently as 1993 were a one-dimensional team with a wild young quarterback in Brett Favre and his one-weaponed passing attack of Sterling Shape. Now Favre is the toast of the NFL, the league's MVP, and he has probably the most impressive array of weapons in the league, ranging from Antonio Freeman to Andre Rison to Keith Jackson and Mark Chmura, to their incomparable return man, Desmond Howard.

Almost every week this season one or several have stepped forward, and the NFL's biggest showcase was no different. Freeman and Rison caught long touchdown passes, Howard was at his back-breaking best, and Favre ran the team with precision.

"I think the Packers' weapons now in the 19th week of the season speak for themselves," said Al Groh, the defensive coordinator for the vanquished Patriots.

Desmond Howard's third quarter 99-yard kickoff return for a TD sealed the Packers' win.

Andre Rison scored the Packers' first TD, but couldn't snag this one in the end zone.

Super Bowl XXXI | January 26, 1997

"The highest-scoring offense in the league. It's usually done with weapons, so they don't need me to speak for them I think they've made their own statement here this month."

The Packers finish the season at 16-3 and clearly as the best team in football for this year. With Favre just coming into his own at the age of 27, and with a nucleus of others coming back, Sunday's win begged for a look forward as much as a look back. Could this be just the start of something really big for General Manager Ron Wolf and Coach Mike Holmgren? Or will the possible free agency of players such as defensive tackle Gilbert Brown and linebacker Wayne Simmons erode too much of the talent to keep the Packers on top of the football world for long?

"Our guys have done an excellent job. Ron Wolf and Mike and the people in personnel have done a great job of evaluating talent," said Sherman Lewis, the Packers' offensive coordinator. "We're going to lose some good players, but we'll also acquire some. As long as we have the quarterback and a good, sound defense, we will be competitive. But to get this far you have to have a little luck, too."

Just how good were these Packers? They finished the regular season as both the highest-scoring and stingiest team in the NFL. They needed both against a Patriots team that had some quick-strike offense of its own that turned a 10-0 Packers lead into a 14-point deficit in a four-minute stretch late in the first quarter. That threatened to give the Packers' dream season a terribly bitter ending.

But the Packers' punch was too much. Favre finished the day 14-for-27 passing for 246 yards, two touchdowns and no interceptions. Most of those yards came on two scintillating plays: An audibled 54-yard TD to Rison on the Packers' second play, and an 81-yard TD to Freeman that put the Packers back ahead, 17-14, less than a minute in the second quarter.

Game 19: Super Bowl XXXI

New England	14	0	7	0	21
Green Bay	10	17	8	0	35

1st Quarter: GB: Rison 54-yard pass from Favre (Jacke kick) (3:32).
GB: Jacke 37-yard field goal (6:18).
NE: Byars 1-yard pass from Bledsoe (Vinatieri kick) (8:25).
NE: Coates 4-yard pass from Bledsoe (Vinatieri kick) (12:27).
2nd Quarter: GB: Freeman 81-yard pass from Favre (Jacke kick) (:56).
GB: Jacke 31-yard field goal (6:45).
GB: Favre 2-yard run (Jacke kick) (13:49).
3rd Quarter: NE: Martin 18-yard run (Vinatieri kick) (11:33).
GB: Howard 99-yard kickoff return (Chmura pass from Favre) (11:50).
4th Quarter: No scoring
Attendance: 72,301

	GB	NE
First downs	16	16
By rushing	8	3
By passing	6	12
By penalties	2	1
Punts/average	7-42.7	8-45.1
Sacks/yards lost	5-38	5-39
Penalties/yards	3-41	2-22
Fumbles/lost	0-0	0-0
3rd down efficiency	3-15	4-14
4th down efficiency	0-1	0-2
Field goals	2-3	0-0
Extra points (kicking)	3-3	3-3
Return yards	244	165

Throw in Howard's 99-yard kickoff return for a touchdown that won him the game's MVP award, and the flurry was more than the Patriots could withstand. It also invited comparisons to the team that this Packers' club is in some ways patterned — the San Francisco 49ers clubs that Holmgren and Lewis worked for as assistant coaches. Those teams won back-to-back Super Bowls in 1988 and '89 with offenses as good as the game has ever seen.

As impressive as these Packers have been, they can't yet be put in that class.

"That team had a lot of weapons," Lewis said. "We had Jerry Rice and John Taylor and Brent Jones and Roger Craig and Joe Montana. Talk about some talent."

If Rison's TD got the Packers off to a smoking start and Freeman's a quick rebound from the Patriots' surprisingly quick comeback, Howard's might have been the biggest. New England had stopped the Packers on fourth down on their initial second-half possession, and then the Patriots got a TD of their own that cut the Packers' lead to 27-21.

But Howard slammed the door on the very next play and in some ways ended the contest right there with his 99-yard score.

"Up until that point, I thought we still had an opportunity," said Patriots coach Bill Parcells.

The Patriots had two big plays in the first half — a 26-yard pass interference penalty that receiver Shawn Jefferson drew from cornerback Craig Newsome, and a 44-yard pass to Terry Glenn. The penalty set up a 1-yard TD pass from Bledsoe to Keith Byars, and the Glenn catch set up a 4-yard TD pass to Ben Coates.

But in the second half, Martin ran for only 42 yards, so New England was unable to control the clock, and four Packers intercepted Bledsoe — Newsome, Doug Evans, Mike Prior and Brian Williams.

That kept the Packers comfortably ahead for most of the second half and gave them time to celebrate the championship they will hold for at least a year.

"We had the better team," Lewis said. "It's as simple as that."

Brett Favre celebrates his diving TD in the second quarter amidst a controversial official's call.

Good Guys Finish First

BY CHRIS HAVEL
Press-Gazette

The doubters have been silenced. The demons have been exorcised.

The Green Bay Packers stand today as Super Bowl champions, having secured a special place in history with Sunday's 35-21 victory over New England.

It is difficult to imagine a more deserving outfit than this. Good guys can, and do, finish first. Selflessness has been rewarded.

The Packers greeted the finality of this job well done with the maturity that is forged through adversity. Their success wasn't accorded. It was earned. While so many members of this team had their own private battles to fight, they stuck together to reach a common goal.

"I look at the faces of my players and my coaches and ownership in the locker room and I'm humbled by that, overwhelmed by it," Coach Mike Holmgren said. "There is a great sense of accomplishment. I'm so happy for these guys. They've worked so very, very hard for this."

Let the roll call begin.

There is Reggie White, the Minister of Defense, who now has a ring to match his faith. If anyone still doubts whether his skills have eroded at 35, go ask the Patriots' Max Lane. He'll be the guy with the bruises. White tossed him aside like a 300-pound rag doll en route to three sacks.

"It's complete," White said of his long journey to the top. "But I still have a few more years. I wouldn't mind having another (ring)."

White's eyes welled with tears when he spoke of the camaraderie on this team.

"There are no individuals on this team," he said. "It feels good to on a team that works toward the same goals. To be with guys who are unselfish. This is probably the first team that I've been on where you actually enjoyed coming to work each day."

There is Sean Jones, the controversial old Raider and Oiler who found both a home and happiness in Green Bay.

"A lot of guys questioned our heart and our ability, so it's good to finally win this game and shut a lot of people up," Jones said. "We're not flashy. We're not flamboyant. But we won it. And the rest of them were sitting home."

Brett Favre's road to Super Bowl XXXI wasn't exactly a joy ride.

There was a pain killer addiction to overcome, the death of good friend Mark Haverty to endure and the string of family problems to deal with. After the game, Favre's thoughts turned to Haverty, who died in an offseason car-train accident.

"I love Mark's family and I know this will help them," Favre said. "We've all been through a lot together."

Asked about his family and friends in Kiln, Miss., Favre replied, "Amen to them. I only wish I could've been there all week to enjoy it with them."

The victory left defensive coordinator Fritz Shurmur at a loss for words, no small feat when you consider this five-time author's command of the English language.

"After 43 years, and that's a pretty long time, this moment is the highlight, but it's hard to describe," he said. "I'd search for words, but I don't think I'd do it justice."

Shurmur, who is 65 going on 35, threw everything he had at the pesky Patriots. The 4-3. The 3-3. The

The Prize: Packers' defensive end Sean Jones, while holding his son while admiring the Lombardi Trophy.

3-4. Shurmur used every conceivable configuration of 11 players to knock out New England.

"I credit our players for that," he said modestly.

The Packers performed in Super Bowl XXXI just like they have all season.

Favre used his smarts (he audibled on the 54-yard touchdown to Andre Rison) and his arm (he threw a bullet to Antonio Freeman for the 81-yard score) to capture this win.

Desmond Howard used his moves and his blocks to break the Patriots' backs.

The defense was relentless. It gave up three touchdowns, but when you consider the Patriots' arsenal, it wasn't too shabby. Said safety Eugene Robinson, "LeRoy Butler said it best. 'Don't look for the next guy to do it. You do it.'"

And so the Packers did.

Finally, after so many seasons of suffering, they have restored the "Title" in "Titletown." It couldn't have happened to better bunch.

The Comeback Kids

By Chris Havel
Press-Gazette

Desmond Howard barely survived the training camp cutdown. Andre Rison was a waiver-wire acquisition at midseason.

Together, these erstwhile castoffs came up with the key plays that led the Packers to a convincing 35-21 victory over New England in Super Bowl XXXI.

"That's why Ron Wolf is Ron Wolf," said running back Edgar Bennett, referring to the Packers' general manager. "He takes chances on players when other teams give up on them. He knows talent when he sees it and he isn't afraid to do whatever it takes to help the team."

Wolf coveted Howard in the 1992 NFL draft, but the former Michigan star was snatched up by the Redskins just ahead of Green Bay. Four years later, Wolf signed Howard after the Redskins and Jaguars believed he was finished.

The payoff came Sunday. Howard, the former Heisman Trophy winner, made the Patriots' cover guys look like statues. His record-setting, 99-yard kickoff return for a touchdown in the third quarter broke the Patriots' backs. New England had just closed to within 27-21 when Howard struck.

The shifty return ace finished with 244 return yards to earn Most Valuable Player honors. He became the first special teams player to be so honored in Super Bowl history.

"There's an old saying that the cream always rises to the top," Howard said. "I was just another strong link in this very, very strong chain. You have such talent on this team, you just want to contribute."

Howard, who set the NFL's single-season punt return record this year, wasn't surprised by his big day. He was surprised the Patriots decided to kick it to him.

"They can roll the dice and kick it to me if they want, but I have full confidence in my return team," he said. "I knew they were going to allow me to pop one sooner or later because they did it all year long."

Then there is the man they call "Bad Moon." He proved to be bad news for New England.

Rison, the wayward wideout, turned the Patriots' defensive backs inside out. When Otis Smith, the Patriots' overmatched right cornerback, wasn't grasping at air, he was gasping for it.

Rison struck on the Packers' second play from scrimmage when he juked Smith at the line and hauled in Brett Favre's pass for a 54-yard touchdown. It set the tone in a frenzied first half and served notice that Rison meant business in his first Super Bowl appearance.

Offensive coordinator Sherman Lewis said Favre audibled to what they call a "razor."

"It's a post and shake," Lewis said. "And Andre hit the post. They blitzed us, Brett read it and they had no free safety, so it was Andre one-on-one with the corner and he beat him."

Interestingly, Rison said he was nervous before the game.

"When I was warming up I had knots in my stomach and that's the first time I've ever had knots," he said. "That let me know how big a game this was. I just asked the Lord for guidance.

"And I know I have the ability to play this game and play it well."

Rison finished with two catches for 77 yards.

The big game cemented Rison's place in the hearts of his teammates and fans.

Rison's influence was felt in the Packers' locker

Antonio Freeman outraces the Patriots' defense for an 81-yard touchdown.

room even before he arrived. Moments after a disheartening 21-6 loss at Dallas, word spread that Jacksonville had placed the 29-year-old receiver on waivers and that Wolf was interested.

The Packers' offense was badly in need of a spark after losing starting flanker Robert Brooks to a season-ending knee injury Oct. 14. Rison was able to provide it.

"I think maybe I added some confidence," he said. "I think it might've been stripped some because of the losses to Kansas City and Dallas, but Green Bay knew it was getting a bona-fide receiver. To the rest of the world, I wasn't a bona-fide receiver. But to the Packers I was, and I'd like to take my hat off to them for giving me a chance to become Andre Rison again. But this time, it's Andre Rison as a better person."

Don Beebe (82), John Michels (77) and Mark Chmura celebrate Antonio Freeman's record 81-yard TD.

Summaries | REGULAR SEASON

Game 1

Green Bay	10	14	10	0	34
Tampa Bay	0	3	0	0	3

1st Quarter: GB: Jacke 23-yard field goal (9-31, 4:26)

GB: Jackson 1-yard pass from Favre (Jacke kick) (2-27, 0:57)

2nd Quarter: TB: Husted 48-yard field goal(11-33, 5:02)

GB: Jackson 4-yard pass from Favre (Jacke kick) (14-82, 6:55)

GB: Jackson 51-yard pass from Favre (Jacke kick) (1-51, 0:10)

3rd Quarter: GB: Jacke 40-yard field goal (9-42, 5:08)

GB: Levens 1-yard pass from Favre (Jacke kick) (4-45, 2:13)

4th Quarter: No scoring

Attendance: 54,102

	GB	TB
First downs	24	15
By rushing	8	4
By passing	15	8
By penalty	1	3
Punts/average	2-44.5	3-46.3
Sacks/yards lost	1-4	1-6
Penalties/yards	6-40	3-20
Fumbles/lost	3-2	3-2
3rd down efficiency	7-13	2-10
4th down efficiency	0-0	1-1
Field goals	2-3	1-1
Extra points (kicking)	4-4	0-0
Return yards	110	0

Game 2

Philadelphia	0	7	0	6	13
Green Bay	10	20	7	2	39

1st Quarter: GB: Jacke 29-yard field goal (4-3, 1:46)

GB: R.Brooks 25-yard pass from Favre (Jacke kick) (5-57, 2:58)

2nd Quarter: GB: Jacke 44-yard field goal (4-6, 1:29)

GB: Levens 1-yard run (Jacke kick) (6-77, 3:02)

PHI: Watters 1-yard run (Anderson kick) (7-93, 3:22)

GB: R.Brooks 20-yard pass from Favre (Jacke kick) (9-72, 1:30)

3rd Quarter: GB: Bennett 25-yard pass from Favre (Jacke kick) (12-82, 7:04)

4th Quarter: GB: Safety Peete sacked by S.Dotson and White

PHI: Garner 1-yard run (pass failed) (16-80, 6:02)

Attendance: 60,666

	GB	PHI
First downs	23	14
By rushing	10	5
By passing	11	7
By penalty	2	2
Punts/average	3-54.7	5-48.4
Sacks/yards lost	1-0	3-12
Penalties/yards	5-23	8-49
Fumbles/lost	2-0	1-1
3rd down efficiency	8-15	3-12
4th down efficiency	0-1	1-1
Field goals	3-3	0-0
Extra points (kicking)	4-4	1-1
Return yards	36	14

Game 3

San Diego	3	0	0	7	10
Green Bay	7	14	7	14	42

1st Quarter: GB: E. Bennett 10-yard run (Jacke kick) (6-55, 3:31)

SD: Carney, 43-yard field goal (10-55, 5:05)

2nd Quarter: GB: Freeman 19-yard pass from Favre (Jacke kick) (6-80, 3:13)

GB: Henderson 8-yard pass from Favre (Jacke kick) (17-88, 9:24)

3rd Quarter: GB: Jackson 7-yard pass from Favre (Jacke kick) (9-50, 5:27)

4th Quarter: SD: Martin 9-yard pass from Humphries (Carney kick) (4-26, 1:18)

GB: Butler 90-yard interception return (Jacke kick)

GB: Howard 65-yard punt return (Jacke kick)

Attendance: 60,584

	GB	SD
First downs	23	11
By rushing	8	1
By passing	14	7
By penalty	1	3
Punts/average	3-38	7-51.9
Sacks/yards lost	1-14	5-36
Penalties/yards	10-90	8-55
Fumbles/lost	2-1	2-1
3rd down efficiency	9-15	2-12
4th down efficiency	0-0	0-0
Field goals	0-1	1-2
Extra points (kicking)	6-6	1-1
Return yards	208	9

Game 4

Green Bay	7	0	14	0	21
Minnesota	7	7	3	13	30

1st Quarter: GB: Brooks 13-yard pass from Favre (Jacke kick) (3-11, 0:54)

MIN: Reed 26-yard pass from Moon (Sisson kick) (4-39, 2:07)

2nd Quarter: MIN: Ismail 20-yard pass from Moon (Sisson kick) (3-4, 0:50)

3rd Quarter: MIN: Sisson 34-yard field goal (11-57, 5:22)

GB: Beebe 80-yard pass from Favre (Jacke kick) (1-80, 0:20)

GB: Koonce 75-yard interception return (Jacke kick)

4th Quarter: MIN: R.Smith 37-yard run (Sisson kick) (7-80, 3:55)

MIN: Sisson 44-yard field goal (4-2, 1:28)

MIN: Sisson 33-yard field goal (4-1, 1;05)

Attendance: 64,168

	GB	MIN
First downs	8	18
By rushing	2	3
By passing	5	15
By penalty	1	0
Punts/average	8-47.5	6-45.8
Sacks/yards lost	7-41	2-17
Penalties/yards	8-79	7-45
Fumbles/lost	5-3	2-2
3rd down efficiency	1-11	9-20
4th down efficiency	0-1	0-0
Field goals	0-0	3-3
Extra points (kicking)	3-3	3-3
Return yards	175	73

Game 5

Green Bay	10	7	7	7	31
Seattle	0	7	3	0	10

1st Quarter: GB: Freeman 13-yard pass from Favre (Jacke kick) (5-46, 2:21)

GB: Jacke 36-yard field goal (4-2, 1:33)

2nd Quarter: GB: Levens 4-yard pass from Favre (Jacke kick) (7-28, 3:04)

SEA: Warren 37-yard run (Peterson kick) (5-73, 1:58)

3rd Quarter: GB: Jackson 10-yard pass from Favre (Jacke kick) (9-77, 4:44)

SEA: Peterson 44-yard field goal (7-53, 2:49)

4th Quarter: GB: Freeman 4-yard pass from Favre (Jacke kick) (5-28, 2:21)

Attendance: 59,973

	GB	SEA
First downs	23	19
By rushing	8	7
By passing	14	9
By penalty	1	3
Punts/average	7-43.4	6-47.0
Sacks/yards lost	2-7	1-1
Penalties/yards	5-37	6-38
Fumbles/lost	1-0	1-1
3rd down efficiency	5-15	4-13
4th down efficiency	0-0	0-1
Field goals	1-2	1-1
Extra points (kicking)	4-4	1-1
Return yards	218	29

Game 6

Green Bay	0	20	14	3	37
Chicago	0	3	3	0	6

1st Quarter: No scoring

2nd Quarter: GB: R.Brooks 18-yard pass from Favre (Jacke kick) (7-53, 3:54)

CHI: Jaeger 40-yard field goal (16-66, 7:15)

GB: Jackson 2-yard pass from Favre (Jacke kick) (9-53, 1:37)

GB: Freeman 50-yard pass from Favre (kick failed) (3-50, 0:20)

3rd Quarter: CHI: Jaeger 41-yard field goal (10-56, 3:43)

GB: Beebe 90-yard kickoff return (Jacke kick)

GB: Freeman 35-yard pass from Favre (Jacke kick) (8-73, 4:42)

4th Quarter: GB: Jacke 32-yard field goal (10-49, 6:18)

Attendance: 65,480

	GB	CHI
First downs	21	15
By rushing	4	5
By passing	16	9
By penalty	1	1
Punts/average	2-36.5	3-52.7
Sacks/yards lost	1-3	1-5
Penalties/yards	4-25	7-68
Fumbles/lost	0-0	1-0
3rd down efficiency	5-9	5-14
4th down efficiency	0-0	2-3
Field goals	1-1	2-2
Extra points (kicking)	4-5	0-0
Return yards	143	152

Summaries | REGULAR SEASON

Game 7

San Francisco	0	17	0	3	0	20
Green Bay	6	0	8	6	3	23

1st Quarter: GB: Jacke 30-yard field goal (6-50, 3:19)
GB: Jacke 25-yard field goal (6-61, 1:24)
2nd Quarter: SF: Wilkins 48-yard field goal (6-36, 1:51)
SF: Rice 7-yard pass from Grbac (Wilkins kick) (8-58, 3:44)
SF: Rice 13-yard pass from Grbac (Wilkins kick) (5-28, 1:09)
3rd Quarter: GB: Beebe 59-yard pass from Favre (Bennett pass from Favre) (4-79, 1:22)
4th Quarter: GB: Jacke 35-yard field goal (15-50, 5:53)
SF: Wilkins 28-yard field goal (4-2, 0:23)
GB: Jacke 31-yard field goal (10-69, 1:42)
Overtime: GB: Jacke 53-yard field goal (7-21, 2:06)
Attendance: 60,716

	GB	SF
First downs	24	14
By rushing	6	4
By passing	15	9
By penalty	3	1
Punts/average	6-39.8	9-41.7
Sacks/yards lost	2-17	1-3
Penalties/yards	2-24	5-18
Fumbles/lost	1-0	0-0
3rd down efficiency	8-20	5-18
4th down efficiency	0-1	0-0
Field goals	5-5	2-2
Extra points (kicking)	0-0	2-2
Return yards	122	188

Game 8

Tampa Bay	0	0	0	7	7
Green Bay	3	10	0	0	13

1st Quarter: GB: Jacke 40-yard field goal (5-10, 1:53)
2nd Quarter: GB: Levens 1-yard run (Jacke kick) (8-63, 3:59)
GB: Jacke 48-yard field goal (13-50, 5;07)
3rd Quarter: No scoring
4th Quarter: TB: Moore 11-yard pass from Dilfer, Husted kick (10-63, 5:33)
Attendance: 60,627

	GB	TB
First downs	24	14
By rushing	11	2
By passing	10	11
By penalty	3	1
Punts/average	2-42.5	5-29.8
Sacks/yards lost	2-9	3-25
Penalties/yards	4-20	6-45
Fumbles/lost	4-1	2-0
3rd down efficiency	6-14	5-14
4th down efficiency	0-1	1-3
Field goals	2-3	0-0
Extra points (kicking)	1-1	1-1
Return yards	62	140

Game 9

Detroit	3	7	0	8	18
Green Bay	7	7	14	0	28

1st Quarter: DET: Hanson 48-yard field goal (11-43, 6:11)
GB: Levens 1-yard pass from Favre (Jacke kick) (14-74, 8:49)
2nd Quarter: DET: Sanders 18-yard run (Hanson kick) (8-68, 3:37)
GB: Mickens 1-yard pass from Favre (Jacke kick) (10-80, 3:37)
3rd Quarter: GB: Mickens 6-yard pass from Favre (Jacke kick) (5-37, 3:26)
GB: Beebe 65-yard pass from Favre (Jacke kick) (4-89, 1:59)
4th Quarter: DET: Perriman 8-yard pass from Majkowski (Moore pass from Majkowski) (9-68, 2:48)
Attendance: 60,790

	GB	DET
First downs	23	15
By rushing	6	6
By passing	15	9
By penalty	2	0
Punts/average	5-31.4	5-37.2
Sacks/yards lost	4-27	5-26
Penalties/yards	8-55	10-91
Fumbles/lost	0-0	1-0
3rd down efficiency	6-12	7-15
4th down efficiency	0-0	0-2
Field goals	0-0	1-1
Extra points (kicking)	4-4	1-1
Return yards	70	121

Game 10

Kansas City	3	17	7	0	27
Green Bay	3	3	7	7	20

1st Quarter: KC: Stoyanovich 26-yard field goal (5-70, 2:01)
GB: Jacke 24-yard field goal (Jacke kick) (12-50, 3:29)
2nd Quarter: KC: Stoyanovich 22-yard field goal (9-75, 3:29)
KC: Hill 8-yard gun (Stoyanovich kick) (5-57, 2:34)
KC: Hill 34-yard pass from Bono (Stoyanovich kick) (4-61, 2:02)
GB: Jacke 49-yard field goal (5-28, 0:56)
3rd Quarter: KC: Hill 24-yard run (Stoyanovich kick) (1-24, 0:07)
GB: Beebe 25-yard pass from Favre (Jacke kick) (8-83, 4:27)
4th Quarter: GB: Mayes 6-yard pass from Favre (Jacke kick) (7-47, 0:45)
Attendance: 79,281

	GB	KC
First downs	24	19
By rushing	2	10
By passing	18	7
By penalty	4	2
Punts/average	6-41.8	7-36
Sacks/yards lost	4-25	1-3
Penalties/yards	7-82	9-81
Fumbles/lost	2-1	1-0
3rd down efficiency	5-14	5-14
4th down efficiency	0-1	0-0
Field goals	2-2	3-3
Extra points (kicking)	2-2	2-2
Return yards	119	93

Game 11

Dallas	6	9	0	6	21
Green Bay	0	0	0	6	6

1st Quarter: DAL: Boniol 45-yard field goal (11:22)
DAL: Boniol 37-yard field goal (4:47)
2nd Quarter: DAL: Boniol 42-yard field goal (14:01)
DAL: Boniol 45-yard field goal (6:30)
DAL: Boniol 35-yard field goal (0:07)
3rd Quarter: No scoring
4th Quarter: DAL: Boniol 39-yard field goal (8:15)
GB: Mayes 3-yard pass from Favre (pass failed) (1:53)
DAL: Boniol 28-yard field goal (0:20)
Attendance: 65,032

	GB	DAL
First downs	15	16
By rushing	6	4
By passing	9	9
By penalty	0	3
Punts/average	7-44.9	4-45.0
Sacks/yards lost	4-30	1-1
Penalties/yards	6-28	5-25
Fumbles/lost	1-0	2-0
3rd down efficiency	4-15	6-16
4th down efficiency	2-3	0-0
Field goals	0-1	7-7
Extra points (kicking)	0-0	0-0
Return yards	14	50

Game 12

St. Louis	0	9	0	0	9
Green Bay	0	3	14	7	24

1st Quarter: No scoring
2nd Quarter: STL: Bruce 6-yard pass from Banks (Lohmiller kick) (2:29)
STL: Safety, Favre intentional grounding in end zone (2:08)
GB: Jacke 37-yard field goal (0:00)
3rd Quarter: GB: Evans 32-yard interception return (Jacke kick) (14:05)
GB: Jackson 6-yard pass from Favre (Jacke kick) (3:59)
4th Quarter: GB: Levens 5-yard pass from Favre (Jacke kick) (14:08)
Attendance: 61,499

	GB	STL
First downs	15	15
By rushing	4	4
By passing	10	10
By penalties	1	1
Punts/average	6-44.3	7-49.3
Sacks/yards lost	2-24	3-5
Penalties/yards	6-30	7-36
Fumbles/lost	0-0	3-2
3rd down efficiency	9-18	6-15
4th down efficiency	0-0	1-2
Field goals	1-1	0-0
Extra points (kicking)	3-3	1-1
Return yards	87	44

Summaries | REGULAR SEASON AND PLAYOFFS

Game 13

Chicago	0	7	3	7	17
Green Bay	0	7	7	14	28

1st Quarter: No scoring
2nd Quarter: CHI: Engram 15-yard pass from Krieg (Jaeger kick) (12-70, 6:34)
GB: Jackson 19-yard pass from Favre (Jacke kick) (4-64, 0:36)
3rd Quarter: GB: Howard 75-yard punt return (Jacke kick)
CHI: Jaeger 35-yard field goal (8-47, 3:16)
4th Quarter: GB: Levens 10-yard run (Jacke kick) (9-80, 4:34)
GB: Favre 1-yard run (Jacke kick) (10-47, 6:01)
CHI: Engram 5-yard pass from Krieg (Jaeger kick) (16-60, 3:44)
Attendance: 59,682

	GB	CHI
First downs	20	21
By rushing	9	8
By passing	10	13
By penalty	1	0
Punts/average	4-40.3	5-40.2
Sacks/yards lost	2-15	1-10
Penalties/yards	2-10	3-30
Fumbles/lost	3-0	1-0
3rd down efficiency	2-9	3-15
4th down efficiency	1-1	5-5
Field goals	0-1	1-1
Extra points (kicking)	4-4	2-2
Return yards	148	80

Game 14

Denver	3	0	3	0	6
Green Bay	3	10	7	21	41

1st Quarter: GB: Jacke 33-yard field goal (11-26, 4:50)
DEN: Elam 40-yard field goal (10-47, 5:08)
2nd Quarter: GB: Jacke 22-yard field goal (13-46, 6:59)
GB: Freeman 14-yard pass from Favre (Jacke kick) (5-73, 0:34)
3rd Quarter: DEN: Elam 39-yard field goal (4-7, 2:00)
GB: Freeman 51-yard pass from Favre (Jacke kick) (8-88, 3:08)
4th Quarter: GB: Jackson 1-yard pass from Favre (Jacke kick) (11-50, 6:05)
GB: Freeman 25-yard pass from Favre (Jacke kick) (6-35, 3:44)
GB: Beebe recovered fumble in end zone (Jacke kick) (3-15, 1:36)
Attendance: 60,712

	GB	DEN
First downs	22	9
By rushing	7	3
By passing	14	6
By penalty	1	0
Punts/average	2-39	5-34.8
Sacks/yards lost	2-15	1-10
Penalties/yards	7-45	10-65
Fumbles/lost	2-0	4-3
3rd down efficiency	12-18	6-13
4th down efficiency	0-0	0-0
Field goals	2-2	2-2
Extra points (kicking)	5-5	0-0
Return yards	65	173

Game 15

Detroit	0	0	3	0	3
Green Bay	3	7	6	15	31

1st Quarter: GB: Jacke 20-yard field goal (10-34, 4:55)
2nd Quarter: GB: Howard 92-yard punt return (Jacke kick)
3rd Quarter: GB: Favre 1-yard run (kick failed, wide left) (8-80, 4:42)
DET: Hanson 39-yard field goal (7-34, 3_09)
4th Quarter: GB: Levens 1-yard run (Bennett pass from Favre) (8-68, 4:55)
GB: Freeman 27-yard pass from Favre (Jacke kick) (9-67, 4:38)
Attendance: 73,214

	GB	DET
First downs	20	19
By rushing	9	4
By passing	10	14
By penalty	1	1
Punts/average	2-44	5-44
Sacks/yards lost	3-15	4-21
Penalties/yards	11-75	7-60
Fumbles/lost	1-0	1-0
3rd down efficiency	5-10	3-13
4th down efficiency	1-1	3-4
Field goals	1-1	1-1
Extra points (kicking)	3-4	0-0
Return yards	204	29

Game 16

Minnesota	7	3	0	0	10
Green Bay	7	3	14	14	38

1st Quarter: GB: Bennett 5-yard run (Jacke kick) (8-66, 5:35)
MIN: Carter 43-yard pass from Johnson (Sisson kick) (10-82, 5:30)
2nd Quarter: GB: Jacke 35-yard field goal (6-32, 2:54)
MIN: Sisson 34-yard field goal (11-71, 1:58)
3rd Quarter: GB: Levens 13-yard pass from Favre (Jacke kick) (6-57, 3:00)
GB: Rison 22-yard pass from Favre (Jacke kick) (9-76, 4:25)
4th Quarter: GB: Jackson 23-yard pass from Favre (Jacke kick) (8-61, 4:43)
GB: Levens 11-yard run (Jacke kick) (3-20, 1:31)
Attendance: 59,306

	GB	MIN
First downs	29	12
By rushing	18	2
By passing	11	9
By penalty	0	1
Punts/average	3-41	8-41.9
Sacks/yards lost	2-8	2-5
Penalties/yards	2-10	5-25
Fumbles/lost	3-2	1-1
3rd down efficiency	5-11	3-12
4th down efficiency	1-1	0-0
Field goals	1-1	1-1
Extra points (kicking)	5-5	1-1
Return yards	104	0

Game 17

San Francisco	0	7	7	0	14
Green Bay	14	7	7	7	35

1st Quarter: GB: Howard 71-yard punt return (Jacke kick)
GB: Rison 4-yard pass from Favre (Jacke kick) (2-7, 0:44)
2nd Quarter: GB: Bennett 2-yard run (Jacke kick) (3-15, 1:45)
SF: Kirby 8-yard pass from Grbac (Wilkins kick) (6-26, 1:22)
3rd Quarter: SF: Grbac 4-yard run (Wilkins kick) (1-4, 0:16)
GB: Freeman fumble recovered in end zone (Jacke kick) (12-72, 7:54)
4th Quarter: GB: Bennett 11-yard run (Jacke kick) (6-32, 3:44)
Attendance: 60,787

	GB	SF
First downs	15	12
By rushing	10	4
By passing	5	8
By penalty	0	0
Punts/average	6-43.2	6-35.8
Sacks/yards lost	1-8	1-5
Penalties/yards	1-5	6-42
Fumbles/lost	5-1	3-2
3rd down efficiency	4-12	8-17
4th down efficiency	2-2	0-1
Field goals	0-0	0-0
Extra points (kicking)	5-5	2-2
Return yards	122	23

Game 18: NFC Championship

Carolina	7	3	3	0	13
Green Bay	0	17	10	3	30

1st Quarter: CAR: Griffith 3-yard pass from Collins (Kasay kick), 5:10 (2-2, :27)
2nd Quarter: GB: Levens 29-yard pass from Favre (Jacke kick), 14:54 (4-73, 1:43)
CAR: Kasay 22-yard field goal, 8:40 (7-41, 3:17)
GB: Freeman 6-yard pass from Favre (Jacke kick), :48 (15-71, 7:52)
GB: Jacke 31-yard field goal, :10 (4-48, :25)
3rd Quarter: GB: Jacke 32-yard field goal, 8:15 (11-73, 6:45)
CAR: Kasay 23-yard field goal, 3:23 (11-73, 4:53)
GB: Bennett 4-yard run (Jacke kick), 1:58 (3-74, 1:25)
4th Quarter: GB: Jacke 28-yard field goal, 10:02 (11-36, 6:21)
Attendance: 60,216

	GB	CAR
First downs	22	12
By rushing	10	1
By passing	12	11
By penalty	0	0
Punts/average	2-36.0	5-36.0
Sacks/yards lost	0-0	2-9
Penalties/yards	5-45	4-25
Fumbles/lost	2-1	2-1
3rd down efficiency	9-17	5-13
4th down efficiency	1-1	0-0
Field goals	3-4	2-2
Extra points (kicking)	3-3	1-1
Return yards	142	100

Photo Credits

GREEN BAY PRESS-GAZETTE - Back Cover, i, iii, iv-v, vii, 8-9, 9, 10, 12-13, 14, 15, 21, 23, 26, 27, 43, 44, 46-47, 48,49, 50, 51, 52, 53, 54, 55, 57, 58, 61, 62, 63, 64, 79, 80-81, 83, 84, 86, 89, 91, 92, 93, 100, 102, 103, 104-105, 106, 108, 109, 110, 112-113, 114, 115, 116-117, 119, 120, 121, 122-123, 124, 125, 126-127, 128, 131, 133.

AP/ WIDE WORLD PHOTO - Front Cover, 11, 17, 19, 29, 31, 32-33, 34, 37, 38, 39, 40, 66, 69, 70, 72, 75, 77, 97, 99, 130, 134-135, 146, 148, 150-151, 155, 160.

REUTERS - 147, 153, 156.